Social Work
in Iran Since the
White Revolution

CHARLES S. PRIGMORE

The University of Alabama Press
University, Alabama

Copyright © 1976 by
The University of Alabama Press
ISBN 0-8173 – 4500-0
Library of Congress Catalog Card Number: 75-9807

Acknowledgments

The author expresses his deep appreciation to the many Persian government officials, faculty members, students and friends of the Teheran School of Social Work, especially the Director of the Teheran School, without whose help and counsel over a period of many months, this book could not have been written nor the accomplishments of the Teheran School of Social Work adequately presented.

The initial typing of the manuscript was the work of Mrs. Shirley Prigmore and Mrs. Soham Gabriel, and Mrs. Karin Rosenberg shared in the editing and final typing. Their valuable contributions are acknowledged.

The suggestions and recommendations made by Dr. Katherine A. Kendall, Secretary General, International Association of Schools of Social Work, by Dr. Ernest F. Witte, Dean Emeritus, College of Social Professions, University of Kentucky, and by Dr. Kenneth Kindelsperger, Dean, School of Social Work, University of Denver, have been very helpful, as have been those of the staff of The University of Alabama Press.

Partial financial assistance was given by the Research Grants Committee of the University of Alabama under Project 614.

Contents

Preface

Coping with change is the lot of all nations in this era of world-wide social upheaval. For a developing country such as Iran, however, change means more than an adjustment to rapid technological development; it means a transformation of social structures and the very life of the people. This book deals with the way in which a school of social work has served as an instrument of social change through its contributions to social policy and its organization of innovative social programs.

Set against the backdrop of the White Revolution, which was personally initiated in 1963 by the Shahanshah of Iran, the author unfolds a story of growing recognition by the nation of the needs of people for a decent existence and basic human rights and services. When the Teheran School of Social Work was established in 1958, there was only one qualified social worker in the country. Such social welfare programs as existed were staffed by untrained personnel. The School faced the enormous challenge of helping a society move from conditions of feudalism into the modern world.

In the background chapters, this volume reveals the nature of the challenge. Prior to the White Revolution, peasants and land were cruelly exploited by absentee landlords whose interests were confined to the income they could derive from their extensive estates. Education, housing, hygiene, or the personal welfare of the people who worked the land were of no concern to the landlords or to anyone else. Literacy, defined as an ability to read the Koran, was put, in 1956, at only 14.9 percent for the entire nation and at 6 percent for the rural population. The rate for women was 7.3 percent and for rural women only one percent. Families were large; women had no rights; men could have as many as four wives; and male children were strongly preferred. In order to keep the peasants ignorant and poor, the landowners opposed the establishment of schools or clinics. Social workers were non-existent in the rural areas and only minimally developed in urban centers such as Teheran. The urban picture that emerges is one of "wealthier people maintaining a good life behind secure walls while the majority lived in poverty, disease, illiteracy, and slum conditions."

From its inception, the Teheran School of Social Work has recognized the need to develop social services that respond to the cultural and social realities of Iran. Schools of social work in developing countries do not, in general, enjoy the luxury of concentrating primarily on the preparation and production of well-qualified social workers. They must give equal attention to the establishment and organization of the services that are required to meet essential needs and to put some quality into the lives of the people.

Two major examples of the impact of the Teheran School as an instrument of social change are outlined in some detail. The programs that developed into a family planning movement and into a growing network of community welfare centers are the product of a common sense response of observed needs and problems combined with a high degree of professional creativity, knowledge, and skill. Miss Sattereh Farman-Farmaian, the architect of social work in Iran and the founder of the School of Social Work, describes the situation faced by the School as it opened its doors in October, 1958.

> That first semester, as we took our students to the field, we saw all the basic human needs which had not been met — poverty, illiteracy, shortage of housing, and disease — and found that we did not have resources to cope with them. We could not very well apply the casework, the psychiatric work, and all the other things we had learned in the United States in Teheran. So, at that time we realized that we had to develop social work for Iran. ("Case study on the Role of Social Work Education in Family Planning,"

New Themes in in Social Work Education, New York: International Association of Schools of Social Work, 1973, p. 192.)

The students immediately grasped the significance of family planning in a situation where girls married young and continued to bear children over a period of thirty years or more. They insisted that the School provide some kind of service despite the fact that family planning could not be discussed openly. The School responded by going underground with the creation of clinics, the importation of teachers and supplies, and the provision of service by the students. This underground movement led, a few years later, to the organization of the Iranian Family Planning Association and, ultimately, to open discussion and acceptance of family planning as a priority concern of the nation.

The community welfare center movement also originated as a direct response to obvious need. In each slum area, students and faculty saw the multiplicity of problems that could be met through an immediately available community service. Working mothers needed a place to bring their children; illiterates needed a place where they could learn to read and write; rural families needed a place where they could learn to cope with urban living; young people needed recreation; and adults needed opportunities to come together for job training or simply to talk with each other. Land has been found and buildings erected for community welfare centers which incorporate day care programs; literacy classes; handicraft and home-making activities; group discussion or activity programs for young people, for men and for women; a playground for children; facilities for lectures and a variety of educational activities; nutritional programs; and clinics for pre-natal and post-natal care and family planning. An interesting feature of the newest of the community welfare centers is that they have been designed to provide aesthetic pleasure as well as community services. Paintings donated by students at Teheran University line the walls; there are goldfish and birds; the rooms are tastefully decorated and furnished; and the grounds are beautifully landscaped. Miss Farman-Farmaian once responded to a comment about the beauty of the center and its surroundings, "Well, it is about time people realized that beauty is not the prerogative of the rich. It is the right of everyone to enjoy pleasant surroundings."

The sweeping reforms brought about after 1963 by the White Revolution greatly enlarged the School's opportunities to pioneer new services and to contribute the growing expertise of its faculty, graduates, and students to the implementation of forward-looking social policies. The substitution for military training of service in a Health Corps, Literacy Corps, or Agricultural Corps has brought an army of young volunteers into the field of social development, which means that services are now being carried deep into rural areas. While the School has, of necessity, worked primarily in the urban environment of Teheran, it has sent groups of students for stated periods into the rural areas and has worked with the literacy, health, and agricultural volunteers to bring new services to the people.

But environmental change is only part of what a school of social work can contribute to social development. In a feudalistic society, hardships are accepted as a natural consequence of living. One does not question fate and one does not expect much for oneself or one's children. Attitudinal change is essential if people are to be helped to better their lot and to participate in the improvement of their lives and the lives of their children.

Through community development programs and in the planning of community welfare centers, the people find themselves, perhaps for the first time in their lives, in a position to assess their own needs and to determine what they want done about them. They become aware of the possibility that they can affect the course of their lives and, particularly, they dare to expect more for their children than fate has decreed for them. The Iranian society is deeply rooted in a cultural heritage of more than four thousand years. It has been a traditional society and old ideas die hard. But, with the impact of modernization, change has come to many in the cities and is coming to many more in the rural areas. Perhaps one of the most significant contributions of the School of Social Work lies in its focus on human development and the capacity of its graduates to help the villagers and the peasants as well as the city dwellers to discover that they can share their own destinies.

This account of the impact of a school of social work on the social policies and programs of a developing country makes it clear that the battles were not won in the classroom. The Teheran School did not neglect the academic needs of the students, but it was in the laboratories of slum neighborhoods, backward villages, and red-light districts that the students came to grips with the problems that had to be solved. With few resources readily available, creative programs were invented to meet specific needs. Out of this experience, long-range plans developed for later far-reaching social movements.

One unmistakable element in the story is the leadership that came from the founder and director of the School. As noted in the concluding chapter, the Director of the School has enlisted ". . . the cooperation of the government officials and legislators to move the nation toward an acceptance of family planning, community development, and care of special groups. . . ." The involvement was complete, with the director learning at first hand from the people what needed to be done and then carrying the message to the highest councils of the nation.

This book tells a story of social change in a developing country that has tried almost overnight to move from feudalism into the modern world. There were many forces at work in the process. One of the most vital was the Teheran School of Social Work. As other schools of social work around the world turn their attention to education for social development and for teaching of social policy, this volume can serve as a guide and a text.

It is indeed fortunate that a Fulbright assignment in Iran made it possible for Miss Farman-Farmaian, the director of the Teheran School, to provide Dr. Charles Prigmore of the University of Alabama School of Social Work with the wealth of information and guidance indispensable for the production of this book. That factual base, enlightened with direct experience, has made it possible to demonstrate through the achievements of one school of social work the truth of the statement in the concluding chapter: "The school of social work of the future can be a highly influential instrument for the planning and carrying out of socio-economic development in a nation or a region." The story in this volume is of interest to all who are concerned with social change in developing or developed countries and will surely serve as a beacon for those schools of social work of the future which see themselves as instruments of social development and social change.

KATHERINE A. KENDALL

Introduction

For some decades, social workers as well as schools of social work have been concerned primarily with services to individuals, families, groups, and communities, despite the early years when the profession of social work was vitally engaged in social reform and social action in both England and the United States. Recently however, in a number of countries, the schools of social work as part of an overall professional effort are playing an increasingly significant role in the implementation of national development, legislation, social institutional change, and other aspects of social action and reform at the societal level.

Iran is one of these countries. At a fortunate time, when extensive economic reforms were underway, the Teheran School of Social Work and its Director were significantly involved in many social developments stemming from the White Revolution and helped to give the impetus behind numerous laws, services, and policies. Perhaps no other school of social work in the world has assumed so forceful a role as an agent for coping with social change resulting from modernization.

This book is devoted to a discussion of the social changes shared in by the Teheran School of Social Work, and the techniques and methods its faculty and students used, in illustration of how social workers can become agents of social change.

It should also be noted that other national forces and professions played significant roles in social developments in Iran. The focus of this book on the role of social work and social work education should in no way detract from an appreciation of the influences and impact of these other groups.

Iran and its White Revolution

The first four chapters provide a background on the social conditions in Iran before and during the White Revolution, and offer some projections of the kinds of changes occurring in social institutions as a result of the White Revolution.

The next four chapters discuss the social responses, including various social welfare policies and services, that have been made to cope with these changes in social institutions and conditions. These policies, programs, and services include development of family planning services, establishment of community welfare centers, and the development of other social services in the urban and rural areas. Primary attention is given to those policies, programs, and services that have had a substantial input from the new social work profession in Iran and specifically from the Teheran School of Social Work.

Part B discusses in detail the history, development, staffing, and problems of the Teheran School of Social Work. Part C focuses on the specific contribution of Miss Sattareh Farman-Farmaian to social change within the White Revolution.

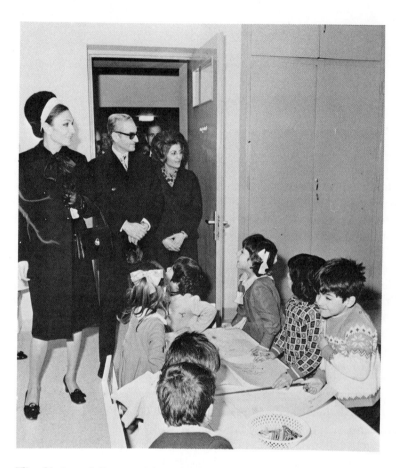

The Shah and Queen visit a children's art class.

I   The Setting and
the People

Geographic, historical, and cultural features distinguish Iran from
its Middle Eastern neighbors. An area of 628,000 square miles and
an estimated population of 31,000,000 make it the second largest
country in the Middle East in size (after Saudi Arabia) and the
third largest in population, following Turkey and Egypt. Iran,
Turkey, and Israel are the only non-Arab countries in the Middle
East. Iranians are Aryans and the national language, Persian or
Farsi, belongs to the Indo-European language group, although
for centuries it has been written in Arabic script. The state religion is Shia Islam, but tolerance of religious minorities is a tradition of long-standing.[1] As a religion, Shiism is ethical and specula-
tive.[2] Religion has been important in Iran, and most social movements have occurred in religious guise or with religious support.[3]
Even today, the government is involving religious authority in
launching modern social and economic programs.[4]

About one-half to two-thirds of the country's population be
longs to the Persian ethnic group and the remainder are primarily
of various Turkish and Arab ethnic origins. There is a sizeable
Turkish minority concentrated in the northwest province of
Azerbaijan and among the tribespeople. About one-fifth of
the population speaks a Turkish dialect called "Azari." An estimated 15 percent of the population belong to tribes, although
most of them are no longer migratory and have settled in towns
and villages. The major tribes are the Kurds, Lurs, Baluchis, Ba-
khtiari, Qashqai, and Khamseh.

Iran's geography has played an important role in its history
and politics. As part of the land bridge between Europe and Asia,

the Iranian plateau has served as a crossroad for great population movements. In prehistoric times, the Indo-European tribes are thought to have passed through Iran on their way to India and Europe and around 2,000 B.C. Aryan tribes made Iran their homeland.[5] The term "Iran" is believed to mean "land of the Aryans." One of these Aryan trbies, the Pars, lent its name to the province of Fars in southcentral Iran and also to the alternate designation of the country, Persia,[6] used in Europe since the Greeks stopped the expansion of the Achaemenian Empire that had originated in the Province of Fars.[7]

Several Iranian cities, notably Teheran, Hamadan, and Isfahan, lie on the east-west trade route, or silk route, which has connected Mesopotamia and China from early times. This has also been the route of successive invasions—by the Greeks, Arabs, Mongols, Turks, and Afghans.[8] In addition to leaving behind diverse population groups, these conquests have produced a culture blended of elements from Central Asia, ancient Greece, the Arab world, India, China, and the West dominated by native Persian culture and traditions.[9] Only two conquests have come from the west—the Greek and the Islamic—while the northeastern border which lacks natural defenses has been breached most often and to devastating effect. With the exception of the Greeks, all the conquerors have been tribespeople who have despoiled urban centers and disrupted agrarian settlements. Many of these tribespeople settled in Iran and took up Persian ways, while others joined the nomads and retained their tribal customs.[10]

Although the various conquerors were often absorbed culturally, the country remained fragmented politically, with a resultant political instability and social insecurity. In its political organization, Iran has fluctuated between fragmentation and centralization achieved by powerful kings. Cyrus the Great was the first to unify the country 2,500 years ago with the establishment of the Achaemenian Empire.

Majid Tehranian characterizes contemporary Iran as heir to four political traditions: the pre-Islamic imperial tradition, the Islamic tradition, the semi-colonial tradition, and the constitutional tradition. The empires of the pre-Islamic tradition gave Iran the monarchial system which rests on the authority of a "king of kings," the *shahanshah*. The combination of Islam, brought to Iran by the Arabs, with the Persian imperial tradition gave the world the Muslim empires. While Iran played an important role in the administration of the empire, it retained its own linguistic, cultural, and national identities. Anglo-Russian rivalry in the nineteenth century reduced Iran to semi-colonial status, and finally a constitutional movement led to the adoption of a constitution in 1905 and the introduction of western political institutions of parliamentary democracy. Like Turkey, but unlike most of the Arab world, Iran remained formally independent under the impact of the West, thus escaping the psychological and political fetters of colonialism and maintaining a more distinct sense of national identity. Iran's social and economic modernization has largely been initiated from above by the country's two most recent rulers, Reza Shah the Great, the founder of the Pahlavi dynasty, and his son, Mohammad Reza Shah. The rapid modernization has been financed primarily by the country's vast oil resources through a series of economic development plans.

The constitution of Iran was ratified in two parts in 1906 and 1907 and its fundamental laws declare the regime to be a constitutional monarchy with the shah as chief of state. He is the commander-in-chief of the armed forces, ratifies laws, inaugurates the Houses of Parliament and is empowered to dissolve them, appoints half of the senators, and signs the treaties. All powers of the realm are declared by the constitution to emanate from the people. The legislative branch of the government is composed of a Majlis and a Senate. In 1973 the Majlis consisted of 268 deputies elected every four years. The number of Majlis members changes periodically, as there is one deputy for every 100,000 people. The Senate is composed of sixty members. Executive power is held by the cabinet. The prime minister and cabinet members are appointed and dismissed by royal decree, but they are individually and collectively responsible to the Parliament, which is entitled to recommend removal by a vote of no-confidence.[11]

Iran's size and natural barriers, including three mountain ranges, and two deserts, have in the past worked against the establishment of a central authority. Most of the country is a high plateau some 4,000 feet above sea level. The Zagros mountains, which run from the northwest southwards, and the Elburz, which separate the lush forests of the Caspian coast from the interior deserts, stamp the form of a V on the country. Most of the country's population is concentrated on the perimeters of the mountains.[12]

The climatic variations in Iran are enormous and while one part of the country may be receiving snow, another may be suffering from temperatures in excess of 100°. Rainfall, too, varies widely, from an average of 50 inches per year for the Caspian area to less than 11 inches for the country as a whole. Approximately one-sixth of the country is barren desert.[13] Two-thirds of the land is unsuitable for cultivation, yet about half of the people depend on the land for their livelihood. Not more than 12 percent of the land is under cultivation. The availability of water, in scarce supply in most of the country, largely determines where people live. The heaviest rainfall is along the Caspian Sea and in the Northwest, and these are the best farming regions. In the interior of the country, villages tend to be at the bases of mountains where water is supplied by mountain streams.[14]

About 60 percent of Iran's approximately 31 million people still live in rural areas (locations with fewer than 1,000 people) as opposed to 69 percent in 1956.[15] Twenty-five years ago, about three-quarters of the economically active population lived in rural areas and was engaged in agriculture, but from 1946 onwards Iran's economy and social structure underwent a substantial transformation. It is estimated that in 1973, 46 percent of the people were engaged in agriculture, 26 percent in industry, and 28 percent in other fields (services, professions, and technical areas).[16] The average per capita income has risen from $193[17] in 1962 to nearly $600 in 1973.[18]

Considerable migration to towns and cities has occurred in recent years. Ten percent of the population now lives in Teheran, which today has an estimated population of over three million. In 1920 Teheran was a town of about 200,000 people and following World War II it still had only 800,000 inhabitants. Since then it has almost quadrupled and it has doubled since 1956.[19] However, a limited supply of water will probably curtail the city's growth at an estimated population of five and a half million. Other cities in Iran show growth patterns similar to Teheran's and in 1966 over one-quarter of the urban population had been born in provinces different from the ones they were living in.[20]

The harsh climate and scarcity of water, combined with low per capita income, especially in rural areas, and a cultural preference for cereals in the diet, resulted in 1965 in an average caloric consumption more than 10 percent below minimum requirements.[21] According to a 1959 report, almost all Iranians, regardless of social class, suffered from malnutrition.[22] This was partly due to lack of protein in the diet, as well as to the eating habits of Persians. Improvements have occurred since 1959.

II Social Conditions Before the White Revolution*

LIFE IN THE VILLAGES

Before the White Revolution, about seventy percent of Iran's population (about 17 million people) lived in its 67,000 villages, but since the White Revolution, this percentage has decreased to about three-fifths. Social, economic and political life has from very early times been centered in the village. Thus, social conditions prior to 1962 must be understood primarily by reference to the villages.[1]

The Persian peasant in the period before the White Revolution and land reform led a life of extreme poverty in these villages comprising flat-roofed mud huts with a few trees, scanty vegetable gardens, a bit of tilled soil and a few sheep, goats, and chickens. Until recently, the peasant remained practically outside the educational system. He was in a "social and political vacuum" in which the landowner or his agent made all the important decisions. Public disorders were and are rare and all village disputes were solved by the landlord's agent or a village elder, the *kadkhuda*, who also served as the local court. One author notes that only Southern Italy and the Balkans reveal similar living conditions among western peasants.[2]

---

*The White Revolution, discussed in greater detail in Chapter III, is a gradual effort to modernize Iran. Initiated by the Shah, it has successfully sought a great deal of popular support in effecting land reform, nationalization of natural resources, electoral reform, improvements in public health and education, and progress in other areas of the Persian social, political, and economic structure. Announced by the Shah in January, 1963, the overall goal is the extension of social justice to all citizens.

Villages range in size from a few people to several thousand, but if the country's rural population were evenly divided among its villages, each village would have about 250 people. At the top of the village structure were the landlord, his agent, and sometimes the head of the local police. In the middle stratum were small peasant landowners, craftsmen, *mullahs* (religious leaders), and small merchants. The lowest level contained the vast majority, which included landless peasants and workers. As the lowest stratum of society, they have had to show obedience to all those above them, and thus the peasantry developed attitudes of servitude and apathy since they could envisage no alternatives.

The landlord-peasant relationship did not encourage social or economic development, and in fact blocked social mobility. The system of customary practices and Islamic beliefs about submission to authority discouraged any initiative on the part of the peasantry. The landlord decided what property was to be farmed, who would farm it, and what the crops would be. Individual peasants had no political rights and virtually no opportunity to improve their economic or social position in the village.

There is no history of peasant rebellions in Iran. Because their physical deprivations were so extreme and the real world offered so little comfort, the peasants sought solace in the supernatural. When no help was forthcoming from that quarter, they resigned themselves to what they saw as God's will. The peasants submitted to the practices of the landlord, whom they rarely if ever saw, because they believed that fate had intervened and determined the existing order.

The middle and lower levels of village society have had little knowledge of life outside, since they neither left the village nor came into contact with outsiders. Villages were self-sufficient and self-contained and the economy was based primarily on barter. Items not grown in the village, chiefly sugar and tea, would be brought in, and a few men would take the crops to market. Donkeys were the sole means of transport.

Since the villages were small and isolated and the village populations had married among themselves for centuries, most people in a village were related. Family ties were strong and family life became the only protection against the harshness of the environment. The disputes that did develop in villages were primarily family feuds.

The peasant holding, or the area that one plough can normally cultivate, has been the basic unit of the village. Along with a ploughland went the right to use village pastures and to collect scrub for fuel in them as well as the obligation to pay dues to and perform labor for the landlord. Farm crops were generally divided between the peasant and the landlord on the basis of the five factors of production: land, labor, oxen, water, and seed. Since the peasant often provided only labor, he then received only one-fifth of the crop.

Between the landowner and the peasant there was often an attitude of mutual suspicion. The landowner saw the peasant as a drudge who would cheat him of his profits if not handled with severity. In fact, most landowners believed that concern for anything beyond the barest necessities would be taken by the peasants as a sign of weakness. Education, hygiene, and suitable housing were regarded as unimportant, except by a minority of enlightened landowners.[3] These few, it should be stressed, were interested in the health, welfare, and education of the peasants in their villages, and helped to construct schools, improve agriculture, and generally tried to upgrade living conditions.

The exploitation of peasants and land in Iran was aggravated by the lack of a stable landed aristocracy comparable to that in earlier England or other western European countries. Under the Islamic inheritance law, land was subdivided among heirs. Moreover, with recurrent anarchic conditions and dynastic changes, the composition of the landowning class changed repeatedly. These factors, along with the confiscation of land, meant that while landowners as a group might continue to hold the same total area, individual areas grew steadily smaller in size.

A landowner of long standing tended to take a long-term interest in his land and peasants. Self-interest ensured that he would provide some tolerable level of economic security for his peasants, if only to keep them from starving or running away with subsequent loss to his own income. But the new or transient landowner was apt to seek a short-term profit and to exploit the

land and its inhabitants without regard to future productivity
or the well-being of the peasants.

A widespread attitude among this relatively unstable landowning class in Iran was that it was better to own several villages
rather than concentrating on one or a very few. Political power
and social prestige depended more on the amount of land owned
rather than on the amount of income received. In the decades
before the White Revolution, landowners were, in fact, less prosperous than contractors and big merchants, although they continued to try to live on a grand scale and to support a host of
dependents. Extravagance in entertainment and travel, with little
income from the villages, led to widespread indebtedness among
landowners.

Individual estates in some parts of the country included over
a hundred villages. In Azerbaijan, Kurdistan, Khuzistan, Kerman,
and other sections, the land and villages were predominantly
owned by large landed proprietors, and in areas such as Arak,
they owned 75 percent of the land.[4]

Most large landed proprietors were absentee landlords who
lived in the capital or provincial capital. They customarily en-
trusted their affairs to bailiffs who often practiced extortion on
the peasants.[5] In the best of circumstances, they were hard task
masters since their main concern was to raise the landlord's and
their own income. In many cases, the large absentee landowner
rented his property to a merchant or contractor who had no
permanent interest in the property and simply tried to squeeze
all he could out of it.

Not all the villages, however, were owned by the large landowners. Extensive holdings in 1926, including numerous villages
as well as agricultural and pastoral lands, were *khaliseh* or lands
owned by the government. These lands had come into the hands
of the government both through confiscation for back taxes as
well as through purchase and bequests. In addition to the *khaliseh*, there were extensive Crown lands. Virtually all of the province of Sistan, 3,000 square miles in area, belonged to the government in 1926. One author notes that in 1941 Crown lands
included holdings in nearly 3,000 villages of the then estimated
45,000 villages in the country.[6] Subsequently, many of these vil-

lages and lands were sold, but as late as 1953 fifty villages in the Teheran area were still government lands.[7] But before land reform, the Crown lands were distributed to peasants.

Most of the government lands were administered by individuals who were given a life use, or shorter use, with the right of transfer.[8] In effect, the villages were turned over to large land owners who often practiced extortion on the peasants and generally failed to look after their well-being. For this reason, the *khaliseh* of Sistan, which had been rented to local notables, were to be distributed to peasants according to a decree of 1937.[9] However, the distribution did not prove to be entirely effective and by 1949 many large landowners moved back into ownership and control.[10]

Another form of land ownership in Iran has been *vaqf* (pl. *ouqaf*), which are lands tied up in perpetuity, either as charitable bequests or as personal bequests in the form of a trust for the founder's descendents. This institution is essentially Islamic, and according to Islamic law the administrator receives ten percent of the income from the property. Charitable *ouqaf* were set up for the upkeep of shrines and religious schools, the support of religious leaders, the performance of religious plays, and other such functions.

Vaqf land was usually leased, although it might also be worked directly. When leased, its administration differed little from that of any other large rental property. The lessee had no permanent interest in the land, and so no long-term improvements were undertaken and the land fell into decay.

Considerable areas of the country were *vaqf*, including a number of villages owned by the Shrine of the Imam Reza in Meshad, the Sepahsalar Mosque in Teheran, and Shah Cheragh Mosque in Shiraz.[11] The Shrine of the Imam Reza was one of the largest landowners in the province of Khurasan, and it leased many of its properties. Considerable *vaqf* properties, including villages and shares in villages, were in Kurdistan, Fars, Kerman, Isfahan, and the Teheran area.

Although the most productive land in the country was held by large landed proprietors, including the *vaqf* and *khaliseh* lands, some villages were owned by peasant proprietors. The main concentration of peasant-held land was along the southwestern and southern borders of the central desert from Qom to Kashan, in other words in the area least susceptible to cultivation. After a bad year, many peasant proprietors would lose their land to merchants and large landowners. Moreover, since holdings were worked largely as family concerns, they would eventually be broken up by inheritance until they were too small to support a family and finally the holdings would usually be sold.

In summary, all past conditions in Iran—natural, legal, religious and governmental—have favored large landed ownership. When peasant proprietorship occurred, it was in marginal areas and without sufficient capital to ensure a good water supply or to withstand poor seasons. The result was that social and economic conditions in villages owned by peasant proprietors did not differ greatly from conditions in villages owned by large landowners.

A more detailed look at some of the aspects of peasant life will provide support to the above generalizations.

The peasant in Iran was largely landless and had no real security of tenure since the landlord could turn him out at will.[12] Peasants were not encouraged to make gardens since they might then become more prosperous and independent.[13] Even when gardens were allowed, as much as one-half the produce would go to the landlord and, after a period of ten or twenty years, the land together with the garden would revert to the landowner. Often the landowners preferred that the peasants own their own houses so that repairs and maintenance would be the peasants' responsibility.

In addition to paying the landowner rent or a share of the crop, the peasant was also liable to various forms of personal servitude. For example, he was required to transport the landowner's share of the harvest from the threshing-floor to the granary, or he might be required to spend a number of days each year in the construction of buildings, roads, irrigation work, or agricultural labor.[14] He might also be expected to provide a certain number of loads of firewood and certain produce such as hens and butter.

Various additional expenses drained the peasant's income. In some parts of Kurdistan he was required to pay the landowner for the permission to marry.[15] Local officials, including bailiffs, village craftsmen, such as blacksmiths and carpenters, servants, bathkeepers, barbers, and religious classes, were commonly paid from the peasant's share of the harvest.[16]

The peasant's income was further depleted when a third person, the *gavband* or foreman, was interposed between the landowner and the peasant.[17] Moreover, payment for extra labor required at harvest and for special operations connected with such crops as opium fell to the peasant.[18]

The peasant often had to supplement his agricultural earnings by labor on the roads, porterage, and other unskilled manual labor. But even then his life was at the barest subsistence level. Peasants were often forced to sell their crops in advance at low prices. Sometimes the landlord, on the threat of withholding water and seed, forced the peasant to sell his own share of the crop at the landlord's price. In addition to selling when prices were lowest, the peasant had to pay for costly means of transport and buy when prices were at a peak. Debt was a constant state and money was lent only at exorbitant interest rates.[19]

Living conditions included overcrowded houses made of mudbrick with small, dark, and badly ventilated rooms.[20] Windows were often lacking. Furniture was frequently limited to a rough mat or felt on the floor. Warmth was provided by a brazier with cow dung used for fuel. One room often served the purposes of sleeping, living, and cooking; and sometimes animals were kept in the same room.

Water was fetched from a village spring or well, and the same water supply was used by animals and for washing as well as drinking.

Although regional styles varied, a rural village typically consisted of a cluster of one-story mud huts.* Villages in the plains were surrounded by a mud brick wall, which was required until the early part of the century to keep out marauders. No such wall was needed around mountain villages, since many of them

---

*Although the past tense is used in this description of a village in keeping with the subject of the chapter, it should be noted that villages far from Teheran still closely resemble this description today.

were almost inaccessible. Farm land or grazing land began just beyond the village wall. Twisting alleys crowded with houses generally branched off a single main street. Each house had a mud wall in front whose doors led to a courtyard containing the family's primitive cooking and sanitation facilities, as well as any animals they might have. A pool in the courtyard contained the family's water supply, which was used by the animals as well as for washing and drinking. A windowless mud hut stood on one side of the courtyard, with a porch across the front to protect the interior from the summer sun. The family usually lived in one room and the animals in a second. Usually, the village leader (*kadkhuda*) lived in a larger house with a third room in which he would receive people. Meals were cooked on a brazier, using cow dung for fuel, and were served on the floor. The brazier would be placed in the courtyard in summer and in the living room in winter, for it was also the only source of heat.

The main diet of the peasant was bread, except in the rice-growing or date-growing areas. Soup was made by boiling a little meat with split peas. In summer the diet was supplemented with vegetables, such as cucumbers, and fruit in the fruit-growing areas. If the peasant owned flocks, he ate a small amount of cheese and curds. Luxuries were limited to tea and sugar.

Clothing was scanty and ragged and often the peasant owned only the clothes he wore, with perhaps a spare shirt. Clothing was made at home by the women from animal wool. The women wore black trousers, a shirt, and the *chadur* or long, loose sort of cape which was tied around the waist and draped the figure from head to foot. The men wore coarse, loose trousers of blue or black cotton, drawn together on a cord at the waist, and a pullover white shirt and tight-fitting cap. Both men and women wore coarse woven white cloth shoes with rawhide soles or went barefoot.

Outside of houses, the only buildings to be found in the villages were a public bath and a mill or threshing floor for grinding flour. In larger villages, one might find a store and a tea house, which, along with the public bath, provided the only settings for social activity. If there was a mosque, it would be located on the public square and might serve as a school house as well as a meeting house. Other than a few trees in the public square, any greenery was scarce.

A water channel, fed by mountain streams or underground canals, flowed down the main street and provided the larger town water supply. Prosperous households of landlords and religious leaders tended to be upstream where water was clean and plentiful. The poorer households of sharecroppers and laborers used the less plentiful and more polluted water downstream.[21]

Public health and educational services were found only in the less remote areas.[22] Local people were used as midwives and healers; nurses were few and far between. The oldest women delivered babies and the child mortality rate was as high as 50 percent.[23] Medicines were insufficient and often expensive. Opium was the most common home remedy to ease pain from illness, accident, discomfort, or cold, and many villagers became addicts. Disease took a heavy toll: malaria was endemic and trachoma widespread.[24]

Only in villages near towns were there schools and they usually consisted of one room with the *mullah* as teacher, or the mosque might double as a schoolhouse. Formal education was limited primarily to memorizing passages from the *Koran*. Teachers were reluctant to accept rural posts owing to the lack of amenities and it was difficult, if not impossible, for women teachers to go to the villages. Children, in any case, were needed in the fields or to tend sheep or weave carpets. Traditional village education was received in the home and in the fields, with the men serving as teachers. The girl's education occurred in the house and yard. Character training and education in hospitality was given to both boys and girls.[25]

It can be appreciated that the literacy rate for the rural population in 1956 was 6 percent, the overall national rate only 14.9 percent, the overall rate for women 7.3 percent, and the rate for rural women only one percent.[26] Literacy, moreover, was usually interpreted as the ability to read the *Koran*.

Even in the enlightened villages where the landowner provided accommodation for a school and the Ministry of Education sent an instructor, the buildings were dark and cramped and the curriculum and textbooks inappropriate.

No recreational facilities or other amenities existed in the villages. The struggle for bare existence would have precluded such recreation, even if the facilities were available.

EARLY EFFORTS AT LAND REFORM

Modifications of the system of land tenure occurred in 1939, 1947, 1952, 1955, and 1956, but peasants were not significantly involved in the management of their affairs and few basic changes occurred.[27] In 1950 the Shah announced that the 2,100 villages in the ownership of the Crown (so-called Crown lands) would be divided into small holdings and sold on long-term credit to landless peasants.[28] One major reason for this move was to provide an example to other large landowners. By 1958 more than a half million acres had been distributed to 25,000 farmers.[29] The distribution was handled by the Bank of Development and Rural Cooperatives, which collected interest-free installment payments from the peasants. These funds were then relent to the peasants through their cooperatives to purchase implements, seed, and machinery as well as to finance the drilling of deep wells and other improvement projects.

Opponents attacked the program on the basis of the small size of the holdings (the maximum having been fixed at 25 acres of irrigated land or 37 acres of non-irrigated land). They also claimed that loans were not adequate to enable the peasants to farm the land efficiently, resulting in a high rate of delinquencies in loan repayments and enforced renting of lands by some farmers.[30]

The early land reform, however, worked well in the Varamin plains southeast of Teheran, where villages were given an extraordinarily large amount of technical and financial assistance. There, the cooperatives functioned well and farmers' income increased two to four times during the 1955–1960 period.[31]

The lesson learned was that peasants had had no opportunity previously to learn how to invest funds wisely in equipment and improvements, and in fact had had little or no opportunity to make any of the decisions called for in equipping and operating a farm. Technical and financial assistance was perceived as extremely important to the success of land reform.

LIFE IN THE URBAN AREAS

The lack of tenure and the bare subsistence level of village life led to widespread movement into towns and cities in the hope of employment and the promise of a better life. The decades after 1920 were a time of urbanization, particularly in Teheran, but also in the provincial cities.[32] Some progress was made in providing the cities with such amenities as electrification of homes, asphalted streets and wider avenues, and public landscaping. But nothing was done until recently to modernize the water supply system, and the highly unsanitary jubes, or open water ducts, provided the major water supply.[33] Work began on a system of piped, pure water in Teheran in 1950 and in 1955 the first connections were made to houses.[34] The sewage disposal system in the cities was equally inadequate.

Health was poor and malnutrition and intestinal disturbances chronic. In fact, in 1955, 25 percent of all deaths in Teheran could be attributed to digestive disorders caused primarily by malnutrition and poor sanitation. Twenty years ago, it was estimated that 40 percent of children born (alive) in Teheran would die by the age of 15 and life expectancy for the country as a whole was only 35 years of age.

Even in the cities, education was still bound by nineteenth century traditions and was limited to clergy who taught in a single classroom with no governmental or professional control.[35] Since tuition was a matter worked out between teacher and parent, poverty prevented most of the urban poor from sending their children to school. After reading and writing were mastered, memorization of the *Koran* and poetry was the keystone of education. As late as 1920, the fundamental reforms needed to create a modern school system had not been made, and not until 1917 was the first school created for women. Efforts were gradually made in the 1920s and 1930s to pattern an elementary and secondary public school system after the French *lycee*.[36] Secondary schools, generally entered at age 13, were neither compulsory nor free.[37]

High school graduates in 1962–63 numbered only 21,002 (compared to 66,338 in 1970-71). University graduates in 1961-62 numbered 2,582 (compared with 12,566 in 1970–71).[38] The first university, the University of Teheran, was founded by Reza Shah in 1935 and a proclamation issued by him that year allowed women to attend the university as well as to hold government jobs and enter professions hitherto closed to them.[39]

Sufficient urban housing for migrants was lacking. Thus, shanty towns sprang up in the south of Teheran and many immigrants who arrived in Teheran during the winter of 1949, for example, settled in abandoned brick kilns south of the city. It took nearly ten years to absorb these families.[40] The great majority of families, which might mean as many as twelve people, lived in one or two rooms.

The situation in provincial cities was perhaps even more bleak than in Teheran. The structure of society in Kerman, for example, has a clear division separating the upper class from commoners. The very steep social gradient was complemented by a virtually non-existent social mobility. Within each level, social status was based on such non-economic factors as religious behavior and kinship affiliation. Unskilled laborers lived at a subsistence level.[41]

In brief, social conditions for the urban poor did not differ greatly from conditions in the villages, although after public schools were established in the 1920s and 1930s some progress was made toward a higher overall standard of living. The pattern was, however, largely one of the wealthier people maintaining a reasonably good life behind secure walls while the majority lived in poverty, disease, illiteracy, and slum conditions. The southern part of Teheran where the poorer immigrants settled thus presented problems of sanitation, poverty, social inequality, and disease.[42] Sunderland refers to the urban centers of Iran as having a very small and extremely rich upper class, a small emerging middle class, and a very large and deprived lower class.[43]

NOMADIC LIFE

The oldest way of life in Iran is that of the tribal nomads and, while many of them have been settled in towns and villages in the past fifty years, there still are many hundreds of thousands of nomads moving with their flocks from summer to winter headquarters.

The tribes follow their own laws, customs, and values and are under the strict authority of *khans*, the hereditary or elected leaders. The *khans* own much of the land and thus have acted as large landed proprietors, collecting from the tribesmen rents for lands and levies for flocks, in addition to the taxes the tribal chiefs must pay the government. Often the government put into power those *khans* who would be subservient, share the proceeds of office, and keep a division of power through intrigue. Among the results were corruption, extortion, poverty among the tribespeople and backward social conditions.[44]

Attempts made to settle tribes in the late 1920s and 1930s led to demoralization and considerable social and economic dislocation. In 1953 the government established a Higher Tribal Council under the Ministry of Court to improve the general economic, health, and educational condition of the tribes.[45]

Cholera, plagues, typhus, and famine have been much more prevalent in overcrowded, unhygienic villages than among the dispersed nomadic tribes, but even among the nomads they have had some deleterious effects.[46] Drought, in particular, has contributed to severe hardship in nomadic tribes.[47]

In short, social conditions among nomads were primitive and marginal. The bare struggle for existence occupied practically all the energies of the people so that education, health, and other social services were virtually non-existent.

FAMILY LIFE BEFORE THE WHITE REVOLUTION

Changes began to occur in Iranian family structure as early as World War I, and pervasive changes have occurred since World War II. But the traditional family structure and processes outlined below prevailed in rural areas and provincial towns and cities at the time of the White Revolution.

The family has traditionally served as the fulcrum by which the individual related himself to the rest of the social system, including political institutions, employment, education, religion, and recreation. The home is an individual's reference point and his haven of security.[48]

The family was the primary economic unit, both for producing money and spending it. The father served as the head of the family, including the families of married children. A boy would work for his father and learn his father's trade, whether land ownership and management, business, handicrafts, or even medicine. In addition to serving as the chief economic unit, the family was the primary medium for recreation, health care, many aspects of education, and the dispensing of justice.

Women had few rights, their role being limited to childbearing and child rearing, homemaking, handicrafts, and sometimes weaving and agriculture. The rules and mores governing marriages, divorce, inheritance, and child care were based on precepts of the Islamic religion. Marriages were arranged for girls at an early age, sometimes even before they reached puberty. A man could have as many as four wives and might well have another family of which the wife had no knowledge, although according to the *Koran* he had to treat all families equally. Governed by strict conventions and traditions, women's lives were hard. A wife was subject to the will of her husband, and beating was the accepted remedy for a disobedient woman. A man was responsible for feeding, housing, and clothing his wife, but, if he decided not to feed her, a woman had little recourse.

A man could divorce a wife without her permission or even her knowledge. Temporary marriages were allowed.[49] No family law existed to protect the rights of women and children. Because of the lowly status of women, male children were considered superior.[50] Inheritance rights were unequal between boys and girls, the girls receiving only half the amount allotted for boys.

A women's freedom of movement was sharply curtailed. The Persian woman lived solely in the home. The only men she ever saw were her husband and her nearest relatives. Her distractions included visits to and from other women, and to the public bath which was reserved for women on certain days. Women did not appear in public at all until the 1930s when Reza Shah set a new tone by encouraging government officials to bring their wives along to state functions.

Many men held the position that education of women was unnecessary and a threat to the peace of the home. As mentioned earlier, in 1956 only 7.3 percent of all women in the country were literate. Canonic law reinforced the isolation and drudgery of women, and the clergy opposed any reform. Women were not allowed to vote or hold important jobs at the Court or in government. A woman could not even obtain an identification card for her child without the intercession of a man. Without the formal written permission of her husband, a women could not leave the country or obtain a passport.

Both the present Shah and his father, Reza Shah, have realized that a radical change in the role and status of women is essential to any lasting program of social reform, because of the meager horizons allowed to women in traditional Persian society. Reza Shah encouraged education and employment for women. Girls' schools were built by the government and, when the country's first university was opened, women were admitted. In 1936 the traditional veil was banned, and those who did not adopt western dress on the street risked jail. Following Reza Shah's abdication in 1941, however, many women returned to the veil.[51]

The parents of a girl traditionally determined when and to whom she should be married. The condition of women was once such that a late nineteenth century author wrote:

> A wife is in subjection to her husband—a subjection so abject that she does not even dream of the possession of those rights which have been and are being granted to women in Christian lands. She occupies the position of slave to man's pleasure and comfort, and aspires to nothing more. She does not sit down to eat with her husband, but eats after waiting on him. If perchance she accompanies him on the street, she walks some distance behind him. Wife-beating is very common, and is allowed by law and custom. Despising his wife as a woman, and having inbred ideas of her inferiority, the husband corrects her and punishes her as a child.[52]

FAMILY LIFE IN THE TRIBES

The most traditional sector in Persian society is the tribal population. Roles are few and are rigidly defined. Expectations are institutionalized and behavior is predictable. Descent is patrilineal and the male owns all productive property. Although women are more active economically than men, their position is inferior. Rights and duties are not equally shared by husbands and wives.[53] The age of marriage for girls is very low, usually about fourteen, betrothal occurring even earlier. Marriages are usually arranged by the girl's father. The tribesman as a Moslem is permitted more than one wife but only the khans can afford this privilege.[54]

III   The Objectives of
the White Revolution

After World War II, urbanization and industrialization began to have a sharp impact on the predominantly agricultural country of Iran, probably accelerated by the growth of the oil industry beginning in 1909 and certainly influenced by increasing contacts with the western nations. Pressures began to be felt for reform of the feudalistic land system outlined in Chapter II, as well as for revision and modernization of social institutions, laws, customs and life styles. The political, economic and educational institutions came under increasingly sharp scrutiny and challenge by the rising middle and working classes during the 1940s and 1950s.

In a real sense, the internal pressures by the 1950s had begun to force a realignment of the Persian social structure.

After a decade of debate and change, including the consolidation of the central authority, a marked improvement in foreign relations, and economic recovery after the oil crisis in the early 1950s, the present Shah felt strong enough to take the initiative in social, economic and political affairs. Noting the inequality of distribution of wealth and power in Iran, he discarded the traditional sources of support for the monarchy—the large landholders, conservative clergy, and old-style political bureaucrats—and appealed to a broadened base of support among the agricultural population at large.[1] This move was aimed at enabling him to pre-empt the programs of the nationalist and radical political opposition.

In January 1963, on the occasion of a National Congress of

24

Rural Cooperatives held in Teheran, the Shah outlined a broad policy based on six points of action. It came to be known as the White Revolution and later as the Revolution of the Shah and the People.[2] The six points specified the following actions:

1. Land reform.
2. Nationalization of forests and pastures.
3. Public sale of state-owned factories.
4. Profit-sharing in industry.
5. Reform of the electoral law, providing equal rights to women.
6. The establishment of a nationwide literacy corps as part of the national drive against illiteracy.

The Shah further announced that, under the provision of Article 26 of the Supplement to the Constitution stating that the powers of the nation are derived from the people, he would place the six points before the public in the form of a referendum prior to the next parliament.[3]

Before the public referendum was held on January 26, 1963, the country went through several weeks of tension and violence. A leading clergyman wrote the Prime Minister, warning that the government must not interfere with the endowed religious estates, the *ouqaf*. The Prime Minister replied that the peasants who lived and worked on the *ouqaf* were no different in their conditions and expectations than other peasants, and that many overseers of the religious lands were dishonest and corrupt. On January 22, the clergy organized a violent demonstration in the bazaar area of Teheran aimed at terrorizing the public and specifically attacking the popular acceptance of participation of women in the referendum.

On January 23, women teachers in Teheran and women employees of many public and private agencies went out on strike in protest against clerical resistance to change. They circulated appeals to women to vote for reform of the electoral law to open the way for woman suffrage.

On January 24, the Shah went to the city of Qom, the seat of Shia Islam, and personally distributed the estates of the Qom diocese to the peasants.

When the referendum was held on January 26, there were 5,598,711 votes for the program and 4,115 against it.[4]

Six further points were subsequently added to the platform of the White Revolution:

7. The establishment of a nationwide health corps to extend modern health practices to rural areas.
8. The establishment of a nationwide extension and development corps for agricultural modernization.
9. Creation of houses of equity to deal with minor cases in rural areas.
10. Nationalization of water.
11. Rural and urban renovation directed toward environmental improvements.
12. Administrative and educational revolution, the former aimed at minimizing bureaucratic red tape and the latter designed to strengthen vocational training and higher education.

The Shah's Own Position on the White Revolution

The Shah has discussed the objectives of the White Revolution in the following words: "In recent years because of Iran's internal situation and her international position I felt an imperative need for a revolution based on the most advanced principles of justice and human rights that would change the framework of our society and make it comparable to that of the most developed countries of the world."[5] Specifically, he discussed distributing "equally amongst the whole population the rights that had been in the hands of the few." He further explains that "Iran needed a deep and fundamental revolution that could, at the same time, put an end to all the social inequalities and all the factors which caused injustice, tyranny and exploitation, and all aspects of reaction which impeded progress and kept our society backward."

The Shah goes on to discuss implementation of the objectives as follows:

> To realize these goals it was essential that land reform should take place and the feudal landlord and peasant system be abolished; that the relationship between workers and employers should be regularized so that labor should not feel exploited; that women— who after all make up half the population—should no longer be

included with lunatics and criminals and deprived of their social rights; that the scourge of illiteracy should be taken away so that illiterates who did not know how to defend themselves would understand and become familiar with their rights; that nobody should die of disease or spend his life in misery and wretchedness through lack of treatment or care; that backwardness in the villages should be ended, and the underdeveloped villages connected with the main centers of the country, and a general condition in harmony with today's civilized world prevail. In utilizing the potential wealth of the country, we had to observe the principles of logic and justice. The God-given resources of the country, which no citizen had himself created, such as oil, mineral deposits, the fish in the sea, forests and great natural pastures, should not fall into the hands of individuals or corporations, nor should the heavy industries, which determine prices . . . become cartels and trusts. For such people or institutions would, in practice, become the successors of the former feudal minorities or past ruling classes.

OTHER ASSESSMENTS OF THE AIMS OF THE WHITE REVOLUTION

Ramesh Sanghvi describes the purpose of the White Revolution as "to transform the feudal, oppressive social structure of Iran into one based upon justice and human rights. The moribund traditional economy was to be replaced by one that would be progressive and self-sustaining. This basic social change was to be carried out by democratic and non-violent means."[6] Harvey Smith and coauthors view the White Revolution in terms of political dynamics, indicating that the Shah had been dependent on the influence of elitist and powerful families of conservative bent in getting legislation through the Majlis. He felt strong enough by 1962, with the aid of a sympathetic prime minister, to set aside this exclusive reliance on the elitists and to build up the political power of the working and peasant classes.[7]

It appears clear that there were a number of other enlightened individuals who supported the Shah and wanted to build a more democratic and economically stable society, and that by the early 1960s the bulk of the Persian people seemed ready to move gradually toward a middle ground economic and political structure between the feudalism of the right and the socialism of the left. Perhaps in a sense the Shah and his governmental supporters and advisors had little choice in the long run but to develop a more progressive and democratic society, if control were not to slip back to the elitist and feudal families or, alternatively, to fall in a revolutionary upheaval led by radical elements.

Yahya Armajani emphasizes the threat of left-wing dissidents, including young army officers and educated youth, who had lost confidence in the government.[8] Armajani notes that national progress would be impeded without the cooperation of these talented youth, and the Shah could only gain their support by demonstrating a reform program incorporating their aspirations as well as the aspirations of the peasants.

Richard W. Cottam views the White Revolution as an effort to block the recurrent agitation of nationalists, students and middle-class dissidents in the early 1960s by appealing to peasants and the working class, hitherto largely "politically inarticulate."[9] Cottam refers to sporadic rioting that had led to political arrests and the continued use of security forces to quell resistance to the regime.

Progress in Implementation of the White Revolution

The overall objectives of the White Revolution were directed at the more equal distribution of income and wealth and the extension of social justice to all citizens.[10] Such objectives represent profound social change even in modern societies. In a structured and rigid society such as Iran's has been, the objectives are perhaps revolutionary, with stress and strain encountered in their implementation. Fundamental changes seem to have occurred in social institutions and in the outlook and beliefs of the people.[11] Yet, it must be recognized that Iran is a nation with an estimated 66,000 to 67,000 villages, many of them very remote and isolated. One suspects that these fundamental changes are probably most characteristic of the residents of urban areas and of villages within a close distance from urban areas. In the Fifth Plan, the government implicitly despairs of reaching into remote villages with rural development plans, and pushes the establishment of rural development centers serving a number of villages.[12]

Among the principal steps was land reform which moved to abolish the traditional landlord-peasant relationship. Land reform proceeded in three stages. In the first phase landlords had to reduce their holdings to one village and the amount they were reimbursed was determined by the value they had placed on their land in property tax returns. In the second phase, landlords were given five choices: tenancy, sale to the peasants, division of the land, formation of a joint enterprise, or purchase of the peasant rights. The third stage, which began in 1966, has emphasized the formation of rural cooperatives and farm corporations.[13] Lambton notes that the cooperatives were central to the success of land reform.[14] Armajani gives especial credit to the Minister of Agriculture, Dr. Hasan Arsanjani, for carrying out the land redistribution program systematically.[15]

Although land reform has clearly shaken the foundation of feudalism in Iran, it may well be necessary to bolster land reform with educational, political, economic, and social reforms to maintain the impetus.

It was noted by a meeting of experts on social policy and planning in 1969 that land reform will work to the advantage of landowners and sharpen inequalities, unless it is bolstered by rural public works, credit, and marketing and extension services.[16]

The second point, nationalization of wooded lands and pastures, followed the realization that only three to five million hectares remained of the 16 to 18 million hectares of forests that once covered Iran. Pasture lands were similarly being ruined through indiscriminate grazing. Nationalization of forests has led to large projects of reforestation very desirable in an arid and stony land.[17]

The sale of state-owned factory shares, in accordance with the third point of the White Revolution, was intended to broaden the industrial ownership base as well as to raise funds to implement land reform. Shares in government-owned factories were offered to landlords, who were also given the options of direct payment over a 15-year period or investment in agricultural development programs.

A law giving workers a share in factory profits has been in effect since 1964 with the purpose of bolstering work incentive, preventing waste and increasing overall efficiency, as well as raising earning levels.

Iran's electoral law reform was implemented by a decree of March 7, 1963. The new law provided for elections to be held simultaneously throughout the country, with every person entitled to vote being provided with an electoral card. The most significant aspect of the law is that women were given equal voting rights with men.[18]

Points six, seven and eight provided for the formation of various revolutionary corps—literacy, health, and development. These corps absorb the surplus of those eligible for military service, provide essential services to rural areas at a minimal cost to the government and establish contact and communication between urban youth and the rural population.[19]

The literacy corps, in addition to reducing the illiteracy rate to an estimated 50 percent in the 10–44 age group, has stimulated the building of a number of schools, mosques, public baths and water culverts.[20] The literacy corps was particularly necessary to reduce illiteracy since there was a serious lack of teachers willing to work in rural areas. Whereas 70 percent of the people were in rural areas, 76 percent of the teachers were in urban areas.[21] Health corpsmen have helped to improve the sanitation and nutrition in villages, have trained people in private and public hygiene, promoted family planning and provided maternity and child care. The aim of the extension and development corps is to show villagers how to employ modern agricultural techniques and implements in order to increase productivity and reconstruct and renovate rural areas. Richard Frye considers the literacy corps to have been "a most successful project [leading to] great expansion and new developments which are still changing the country."[22]

More than 7,000 houses of equity have been established since 1965 to handle minor cases such as petty squabbles and family disputes in rural areas. In 1968 underground water resources were nationalized, and approval from the Ministry of Water and Power is now required before a well is sunk. Among other responsibilities, the Ministry approves sewage disposal plans before new factories are approved for construction. Rural and urban

renovation efforts have been directed towards environmental improvements in sanitation, health and educational facilities.
On October 19, 1967, a royal edict called on every civil servant to perform his duties with honesty, dedication and speed. This action inaugurated the administrative revolution, designed to end bureaucratic pathologies of various kinds. As might be expected from the voluminous research on bureaucracy in various countries, progress has been slow. The educational revolution includes more use of educational planning, a continuous review and criticism of educational curricula and systems, and attention to the training of professional educators. The keynote in all three thrusts is responsiveness to the needs of a changing society.[23]

By 1971 an assessment of progress noted that the power of the landed aristocracy was gone, and the role of the Islamic clergy had been redefined toward religious activities alone.[24] With an economic growth of 12 percent and labor laws supporting the working population, the Shah appeared to have consolidated a new power base. The campaign to reduce illiteracy was well underway, and attention was being directed toward the rejuvenation of higher education. The White Revolution has remained Iranian in nature, with strong central direction and relatively firm goals but with a flexible methodology.

It should be recognized and stressed that the objectives of the White Revolution are long-range and extensive, and although progress has indeed been made, an objective assessment of progress up to 1974 would have to underline the enormous task ahead. For example, the Fifth Plan anticipates that by 1978 an education network will cover all 45,000 villages with a population of 50 or over. But this may still leave many of the total of about 66,000 unreached. (The Fifth Plan gives this number as a more accurate estimate today than the 67,000 projected by Lambton. Many villages have been merged or reclassified as a result of population growth.) Even though the literacy rate among rural women rose from 1 percent in 1956 to 3.4 percent in 1966, largely as a result of the work of the Literacy Corps, one wonders how long it might require to reach the remaining 96.6 percent of rural women. (However, this percentage represents adult women, most of whom have missed their chance. The children, who account for 52 percent of the rural population, are being reached in larger and larger numbers. In two generations or so, the illiterate population should have dropped sharply.) Similar observations could be made about health, justice, standard of living and income redistribution, to mention a few of the chief objectives of the White Revolution. All this is understandable because change is slow in any society or organization, as a result of such forces as the "conservative thrust" of "collective life." the resistance of vested interests, the "personal effort and agony of people" who have to change, the indoctrination in values and behavior that occurs in all societies and organizations, resource limitations, the pressure for stability and continuity and informal constraints on innovation.[25]

REACTIONS TO THE WHITE REVOLUTION

Gradually the resistance of the landlords, clergy, and other groups whose members lost wealth or power as the result of the White Revolution, has lessened. But sporadic tensions have occurred as the various groups and classes in Iran have made an accommodation to rapid and accelerating social and and economic change. Most of the wealthier people, who formerly valued land and villages as the basis of wealth, have turned their attention to accumulation of money. There is, in fact, evidence that Iranians are increasingly viewing money as the only real source of stability in a rapidly changing society.[26] Much of this money has been reinvested in factories, banks and other activities of a more urban, industrial society. The now more numerous members of the middle class have sought money for the education of their children and for other new services and benefits. They have increasingly emulated western life styles although with a Persian dimension and interpretation.

By the late 1970s, active resistance to the White Revolution appears to be limited to extremist groups and a few reactionary elements in the country. Some ultra-conservative religious leaders are also still resistant to some of the reforms.[27] It cannot be doubted that the White Revolution has now been accepted by the great mass of the people. Many students, however, demand more political modernization.[28] Specific difficulties included the rioting that broke out in the Teheran bazaar area in June 1963. At about the same time dissidence flared in the smaller tribes in southern Iran, directed against government policies and programs. These outbreaks were contained by security forces apparently with minimal force.[29]

SOCIAL WELFARE IN THE WHITE REVOLUTION

The government of Iran has recognized that:

The economic and social results of (social welfare) programs, in addition to the extension of social justice by reducing the gaps existing between various social groups, and improving the livelihood of relatively deprived classes, will include improving the quality of the workforce, encouraging people to save and participate effectively in development activities by means of self-help methods, strengthening the cooperative sense and understanding of social responsibility in individuals, and finally establishing greater preparedness for the acceptance of social reform.[30]

The Fifth Plan goes even further to define national policy as having the twin goals of agricultural development and expanded social welfare directed at lower income groups, with the priority objectives including (as the first two): "a) to raise levels of knowledge, culture, health and social welfare, to the greatest extent possible; b) to ensure a more equitable distribution of national income, emphasizing in particular a rapid rise in standards of living and welfare among low-income groups;"[31] The relevance of the policy and objectives of the Fifth Plan to the directions of the White Revolution seem clear and obvious.

In recognition of the value of social welfare services, the government provides support to half a dozen government social welfare agencies, twelve public social organizations, and a number of private institutions. The government agencies include the Ministry of Labor, the Ministry of Social Welfare, the Ministry of Health, and the Ministry of Education.[32] The public social organizations include the Imperial Organization for Social Services, the Red Lion and Sun Society of Iran, the National Association for the Protection of Children, the Farah Charitable Organization, the Foundation for the Protection of Mother and Child, the National Organization for Iranian Scouts, the Society for Abandoned Children, the Society of Supporters of Medical Centers for Children, Vocational Training Center, Society for Aid to Lepers, Cancer Society and Pahlavi Blind Institution. As indicated in Chapter IX, most of these organizations existed prior to the White Revolution, and their functions will be discussed early in Chapter IX.

Some of the private organizations include Women's Organization, Family Planning Association of Iran, Community Welfare Center of Iran and a number of orphanages, clinics and other institutions.

In the Third Development Plan, 1962–1968, no special status was given to social welfare activities.[33] The thrust of the Third Development Plan was on establishing the basis for large-scale economic development, so priority was given to projects involving the manufacturing, electric power, and construction industries.[34] The Fourth Development Plan, however, specified a gradual effort to transform the social services from a remedial to an institutional or developmental pattern with the stated aim of promoting social justice among the various groups of society.

Specific programs to be strengthened in the Fourth Development Plan included social security, child and family welfare, youth welfare, workers' welfare, rural welfare, welfare and rehabilitation of specific groups and training in social welfare.[35] The heaviest stress of the Ministry of Social Welfare, created in the new Fifth Plan, will be on the social insurances and assistance to the needy.[36]

Two social welfare programs discussed in the Fourth Development Plan illustrate how the government of Iran envisions the aid of social welfare personnel in implementing the White Revolution. Because most points of the Revolution are directed toward provisions of rights and justice to the rural citizens and to urban workers, the programs relating to workers' welfare and rural welfare have been selected.

WORKERS' WELFARE[37]

With the industrialization of the country and the rapid increase in the number of workers, as well as their effect on the country's economic growth, go increasing requirements and social and economic problems which call for greater attention to workers' welfare. Among the efforts designed to improve their conditions in the Fourth Development Plan were the following:

1. The extension of literacy campaign classes in major centers of labor concentration.

2. The establishment of 120 short first-aid courses, with the cooperation of the Ministry of Health, the Red Lion and Sun Society and the Social Insurance Organization.

3. The organization of short on-the-job classes for raising the skill levels of employed workers.

4. The creation of two pilot social education centers with a capacity of 60 persons for the training of literate workers with a view to preparing them for social and trade union responsibilities.

5. The establishment of five cultural and sports centers for workers in five industrial regions of the country, as provided for under the youth welfare program.

6. The establishment of four workers' rest-homes in areas with pleasant climates so that workers and their families may use them for holidays, and the completion of summer-camps for workers.

7. Assistance to the private sector in building 10,000 workers' houses.

8. The expansion of cooperatives and the utilization of modern cooperative methods.

9. The establishment of six workers' social service centers as a pilot scheme in major industrial centers of the country (Isfahan, Tabriz, Ahwaz, Arak, Teheran and Yazd).

10. Increasing the number of group contracts and extending safety and labor inspection services by engaging 100 labor inspectors, labor physicians and industrial safety engineers.

11. Encouraging employers to establish day-nurseries in fac-

tories where the number of female workers has reached the level foreseen in the relevant regulations.

12. The provision through Workers' Welfare Bank and Mortgage Bank of Iran of facilities to extend housing loans to workers.

RURAL WELFARE

Over-population at the rural level and the importance of this vast source of manpower to the national product as well as the relatively low level of income of rural inhabitants make it necessary to pay more attention to the welfare of this section of the population.

The lack of coordination among the various executive agencies at the rural level, the sporadic and unsystematic nature of the services offered, coupled with the low level of technical knowledge of the officials involved, have contributed to the complexity of the problems, especially since the ability of the rural population to participate in development activities has been limited in the past.

In extending welfare services to rural society, one objective is to utilize self-help methods to harness the latent power and inherent aptitudes of the villagers. Productivity would thus increase with the ultimate result of improving the living standards and ensuring the welfare of the rural population.

Until recently, government efforts in rural welfare have by necessity been concentrated on improving the economic welfare of the farmers. Mere distribution of land could not itself improve the conditions of the formerly landless farmers or transform the nation's agriculture. Thus, rural cooperatives were instituted to educate the farmers to make full use of the land reform system. These cooperatives teach improved methods of cultivation, introduce new crops, develop markets and train members in administrative and managerial skills.

Since 1968 the government has been establishing cultural houses in rural areas to serve the function that community welfare centers serve in urban areas. The cultural houses offer health and child care facilities, family planning clinics, literacy, and homemaking classes. They also serve as the bases for local organizations such as houses of equity, rural cooperatives, and village councils. Handicraft classes are being introduced and, in the future, artistic and cultural activities will be housed here. Village worker (*debyars*) are trained in the cultural houses to organize village residents into local societies to work out solutions to community problems. The assistance of members of the literacy, health and extension and development corps is sought in carrying out these solutions. One of the most important functions of these village workers is to educate the villagers to accept change.

IV   Changes in Social Institutions Resulting from the White Revolution

Many studies document the social changes generated when a country shifts from an essentially feudal, traditional society to an industrializing, urbanizing and "modern" society.[1] Iran's efforts to reform land tenure policies, nationalize natural resources, and redistribute economic and political power on a more equitable basis constitute such a shift, and that these reform measures would have pervasive and complex social implications involving changes in social institutions is only to be expected. Because these implications often interconnect and overlap, some repetition in the following discussion is unavoidable.

RURAL-TO-URBAN MIGRATION

Under feudalism, peasants had a guaranteed minimum level of subsistence. But when a land reform program, such as that of Iran, is launched, even the minimum security of the peasants is endangered. Most landlords lose whatever sense of responsibility they had for the welfare of their tenants, and the tenants begin looking around for some substitute basis for economic and social security. With the onset of industrialization many peasants move to urban areas, where the prospects for upward mobility appear to be greatest, although many also remain to take advantage of the redistribution of land.

Since World War II, Iran has had an accelerating migration rate from rural areas to cities, particularly to Teheran. Teheran has had a growth rate of six to seven percent per year since World War II, increasing from 1,512,082 residents in 1956 to

38

Institutional Changes 39

2,719,730 in 1966.[2] It was estimated at 3,100,000 in 1973, and projections are for 5,100,000 in 1977.[3] The cities of Isfahan, Meshad, Tabriz, Shiraz, Ahwaz, Kermanshah and Rezayeh have all had only slightly lower growth rates. These migrants come to the cities ill-prepared to adapt to an urban environment. Their educational level is low and their vocational skills non-existent or, at best, poor. Their knowledge of sanitation, hygiene, child care, diet and birth control are inadequate. Many of them are single men who later send for families and relatives to join them.

Nor are cities prepared to cope with migrants in a society confronted with the shift from feudalism to industrialization. Iran has been no exception. Migrants have often been forced to live in abandoned kilns or quarries on the outskirts of the cities without modern conveniences or facilities. Educational and vocational training opportunities have been lacking.

It is in this context that other countries have developed new patterns of social welfare service to aid migrants in the rural-to-urban transition. The Settlement House movement in the United States, for example, represented an effort to help rural immigrants from Europe find a place for themselves in Chicago, New York and other large cities.

Rising Expectations

Under a feudalistic order the peasant does not generally rear his children to expect more from life than he himself received. The attitude towards life tends to be fatalistic and hardships are accepted with resignation and passivity.

But with governmental and societal commitment to reform land distribution and move toward a higher level of social justice, the peasant's outlook towards himself, his life and his children's future tends to change radically.[4] Once the platform of the White Revolution was promulgated, new possibilities opened up and expectations could change. The former peasant no longer sees any reason why his children should remain illiterate. He begins to develop a new attitude toward civic rights and personal property: why shouldn't he have good schools, health clinics, better housing and food and the other niceties of urban, industrial life? He begins to reassess gradually his ideas about family size, in order to ensure proper education for his children. He strives for a good house in a good neighborhood for his family and is therefore willing to hold down two or more jobs to augment his income. He is more willing to allow his wife to work outside the home. He gradually becomes less bound to traditions, religious mores and the other cultural ingredients of a feudal society. He rears his daughters to go without the veil and may even approve miniskirts as a symbol of the new way of life.

1. Rising rural expectations

In the towns, villages and hamlets, people begin to demand better water, sanitation, roads, schools and other conveniences. If the government does not readily build reservoirs, public baths, sewers and new schools, villagers may build them with their own resources. If towns, villages and hamlets remain too backward and unprogressive, many of the more aggressive citizens are likely to move to the larger towns and cities. If and when the more basic needs for water, sanitation and education are satisfied, then the pressure shifts to electricity, universities, better stocked stores and shops, and better health facilities.

2. Rising urban expectations

Once the higher-expectation mechanism is activated, expectations at any level are not easily satisfied. That cities, with a higher level of conveniences and amenities, might better satisfy these expectations, could be anticipated. In actuality, demands increase in an urban setting: for smaller classes and better quality education; for improved medical care, with physicians professionally educated abroad; for better-staffed and better-equipped hospitals; for services designed for the physically handicapped, mentally retarded, alcoholics, addicts and other special groups; for mass transportation such as subways and improved bus systems; for new highways and streets; for parks and playgrounds; for better fire protection; for better handling of automobile traffic. Each family which has one automobile wants two. Students expect to have cars and often obtain them from newly prosperous parents. The demand for imported clothing rises. People want operas, ballets, concerts and other cultural accoutrements of a modern metropolis.

3. The changing role of women and their rising expectations

Women tend to claim an appropriate share of the rising expectations, not only in terms of material advantages and conveniences and improved educational facilities for their children, but also in terms of their own opportunities in life. Thus, women demand the right to vote, to hold office, to receive salaries and promotional opportunities equivalent to their male counterparts, and to receive higher education and to enter professions. Women have been even less prepared to move thoughtfully and maturely into new roles, since the society has traditionally assigned them inferior status. So the early years are apt to be difficult ones, while women try to balance traditional role expectations with new role expectations. Nonetheless, women have moved into cabinet positions, the professions and business in increasing numbers.

EMERGENCE OF A NEW "ELITE," A NEW MIDDLE-CLASS AND THE "SUPER-RICH"

An elite, characterized by a higher level of education and technical knowledge, is coming into existence, particularly in Teheran where men may hold as many as four or five jobs to attain the income and prestige level the members establish for themselves. The members of this new "elite" include university professors, personnel in government ministries, physicians, attorneys, technologists, engineers and other professionals whose skills are in high demand. Some have their children educated in highly expensive, private education institutions owned or operated by foreigners and then send them abroad for university education. A number of children marry abroad and never return to Iran, often with the tacit approval of their parents.

An emerging middle class has developed from the expansion of the new professions, public bureaucracies, business and industry, and other sectors of Iranian life. The members of the new middle class own automobiles and are buying new homes.

A smaller group of "super-rich" industrialists, speculators and merchants is also emerging. This group includes owners and directors of private companies handling the assembly of automobiles in Iran, the manufacturers of items such as shoes and refrigerators, large merchants, people who hold franchises for foreign automobiles, executives of textile industries and other industries stimulated by the White Revolution, and successful real estate speculators. These people are able to live on a lavish scale, to travel and entertain sumptuously and to maintain large estates. Perhaps a major social function they serve, in Iran as in other countries, is to epitomize the goal of the middle-class Iranian for material wealth and prosperity. The obvious social dysfunction is to create a new inequality of wealth and opportunity between social classes.

The Emergence of a Skilled Laborer Class

As a response to the White Revolution, a new class of skilled laborers has arisen to man the factories and industries in Iran and to handle the construction of homes, plants, office buildings and hospitals. Their expectations have increased as their skills have come into demand.

The New Poor

The migration to cities, coupled with the increase in the middle class, has resulted in the development of a new poor who are bereft of the advantages of feudalism and lack any of the advantages of industrialization. This new poor furnishes a large number of the multi-problem families served by social agencies in the cities.

Changing Family Patterns and Parental Discipline

One of the most marked effects of the rural-to-urban migration and the rising expectations has been the drastic change which family relationships undergo, particularly in parental discipline. The role of the father as autocrat, judge and family head has been seriously eroded. Children are more prone to disagree and argue with parents, especially now that they often have more education and more money then their parents. Girls frequently scorn the veil and other evidences of the traditional female role and adopt more modern dress and behavior, regardless of the attitudes of parents. Youth in general have more money to spend than they can easily handle, and conspicuous consumption is growing in the middle class. Marriages are less often arranged and there is a tendency for girls to enter careers and postpone marriage.

CHANGING SOCIAL INSTITUTIONS

In this shift from feudalism to industrialization, not all social changes occur in terms of individual mobility. In launching the White Revolution and altering the system of justice and the economic system, the country not only accelerated rural-to-urban migration and raised the level of expectations, but also set into motion forces that will inevitably change the social institutions of Iran. Religious institutions are, for example, changing their role in a more pragmatic, materialistic urban society. Religious leaders of the future are likely to become more sympathetic to the new order and less attached to the past. They are beginning more frequently to adopt new methods of teaching the youth. The family will inevitably become somewhat more nuclear, especially in urban areas, although it is safe to predict that the extended family will not quickly disappear. Political structures and processes will also be affected, as more people receive better education and wish to have some impact on decision-making. As a result, a political party system has emerged and, with it, a wider participation in the policy-making process.

THE REARRANGEMENTS OF VALUES
AND PRIORITIES AT BOTH THE SOCIAL AND PERSONAL LEVEL

Basic to all the foregoing social implications is a reassessment of what is the good and the desirable both for the society and the individual. The immediate results of the White Revolution are felt primarily on an economic level as the national income rises and is somewhat more equitably distributed. But, as an individual finds his housing, clothing and other material needs better met, his thinking gradually turns to a reevaluation of his society—its values, its goals, its priorities—particularly in terms of how they affect him and his children. He may, for example, want to see better planning, more attention given to the social services and higher educational standards set.

The Role of Social Workers

As the social implications of the White Revolution became clear, Iran has increasingly turned to the emerging profession of social work, among other professions such as medicine and law, for help in readjustment to the problems of rural-to-urban migration, rising expectations, the changing role of women and the change of parental discipline. Queen Farah and the various governmental ministries actively supported the Teheran School of Social Work in its development of new services to cope with programs for migrants, including community welfare centers. Specifically, she has furnished funds, leadership, and guidance. Similar help and encouragement were provided to the School in developing programs of community development in the villages, social services in urban schools, and services to the mentally ill and delinquent—all of them methods of handing the rising expectations and the social results of rising expectations. Illiteracy classes and family planning programs have been developed by social workers, in response to the nation's interest in improving the status of women in Iran. Juvenile court laws and programs, separate institutional care of juvenile delinquents, child welfare services, social work with retarded children in the schools, and parents' classes have all been developed to cope with the problem of parental discipline and changing family patterns.

Specific details of the role of social workers in responding to the changes occurring in the country as a result of the White Revolution are provided in Chapters V, VI, VII, and VIII. In general, however, it should be noted that many of these responses stemmed from the guidance of the Queen, who from the time of her accession has fostered measures designed to better the situation of the people, as well as from discussions with officials of the ministries and charitable foundations.

It is the conviction of the author that social workers in other countries can enlist this kind of power in support of program development if a clear case can be made for the relevance of the programs to overall social policy thrusts of the nation, if avenues to seats of power can be opened up through interest on the part of influential mediators, and, perhaps of equal importance, if the nation has funds available for investment in social welfare. Iran has had oil revenues available for this kind of investment, and it may be noted that a previous government official indicated to the author that social welfare ventures might have been developed more slowly without oil revenues.

V   Family Planning

INTRODUCTION

It is increasingly recognized that family planning efforts alone cannot be expected to control population growth. In fact, leading students of the subject of population control have tentatively concluded that perhaps the most effective single means of curtailing family size in a nation or region is to raise the level of living. This would increase the number of middle class families in the population at risk. A primary middle class goal is to provide better education, health, clothing, diet, and other amenities to children, a goal which can obviously be best realized if the number of children is circumscribed. The evidence so far around the world indicates that those nations with a large and growing middle class have a lowered birth rate, as families begin to perceive future advantages—economically and socially—for a smaller number of children. As Philip M. Hauser puts it, "there is an inverse correlation between levels of living and present or projected rates of population growth."[1]

Yet, a first step in controlling population in industrializing but predominantly rural and lower class countries is often to develop programs of family planning. While such programs are piecemeal, and residual in the sense that they are usually aimed at specific families already beset by problems stemming from too many children, they do satisfy a need to do something about population growth while economic programs attempt to increase the level of living. And such family planning programs may pave

46

the way for a better public understanding of the need to limit family size.

A sound program of population control would seem to call for allocation of resources to "biomedical research and social research designed to improve efforts to control fertility" as well as for increases in productivity as a path to higher levels of living.[2] The relevance of population control to the objectives of the White Revolution has been stressed by the Shah and the government. It is extremely difficult to attain and maintain a higher degree of social justice and a higher level of living for all the people when the population increases at an annual rate of 3.2 percent. The Plan and Budget Organization, for example, observes that "to achieve the national social and economic objectives, top priority has been given to the implementation of the birth control programme, particularly in view of the fact that mortality rates are gradually dropping as a result of improved living conditions."[3] A brief assessment of the impact on national goals and stability of the population growth can be found in *Area Handbook for Iran.*[4]

The Fifth Plan provides a comprehensive approach to population control by listing a number of policies including raising incomes, improving the welfare of low-income people, developing and utilizing the mass media, relying on education particularly in rural areas and low-income sections of urban areas, expanding the family planning clinics, and continuing the family planning function of the Revolutionary Corps.[5]

DEMOGRAPHIC CHARACTERISTICS

Iran's population was 18.9 million in 1956 and 25.7 million in 1966, according to the national census figures. United Nations Projections show the following growth pattern, assuming constant fertility: 39.7 million in 1980, 70 million in 1995, and 85.5 million in 2000.[6] At the current estimated growth rate of 3.2 percent per year, the population will double in 21 years.[7] If efforts to slow the population increase to an annual growth rate of one percent are successful, an "extremely optimistic" projection made by the International Demographic Statistics Center would place the population of Iran at 75 million by 2050.[8]

In 1966 there were 5,212,803 women of reproductive age (15–44) and about half of them were married between the ages of 15 and 19.[9] In the age group 15–19 in 1956, seven percent of the males and 41 percent of the females were married, and in 1966, six percent of the males and 47 percent of the females were married. In essence, a very high percentage of young girls in Iran are married. This suggests even higher population growth rates, as young marriage means a prolonged period of fertility, a greater number of children, and, with the increased chances of survival, an increase in the youthfulness of the population. Iran has a young population and its youthfulness is increasing. According to the 1956 census, 42.2 percent of the population was in the 0–14 age group and in 1966, 46.3 percent of the population fell into this group.[10]

BACKGROUND OF FAMILY PLANNING EFFORTS

The Maternal and Child Health Clinics, set up in 1953, disseminated the earliest information on family planning in Iran, but they did not provide contraceptive devices. The first systematic efforts to provide clinical services and to change attitudes towards family planning and population growth were made by social workers. The need for a serious family planning program became evident as soon as professional and student social workers began going into slum communities shortly after the opening of the Teheran School of Social Work in 1958.

Once the urgency of the population problem had been recognized, a volunteer group was formed which included a team of eight gynecologists and midwives, a member of Parliament, the director of the Teheran School of Social Work, the head of the Foundation for the Protection of Mother and Child, the heads of two nursing schools and one physician who was the director general of the Maternity and Child Health Division of the Ministry of Health. Later the group was recognized by the government as the Family Planning Association of Iran (FPA), with the director of the Teheran School of Social Work serving as chairman.

Education and motivation in the limitation of family size were the main goals of the organization from the outset. The FPA worked quietly and did not publicize its efforts at first, fearing

repercussions from conservative religious and social groups. At
the time it began its activities, moreover, the priority need was
the provision of clinical services. Although the contraceptive
methods available at that time were somewhat primitive—condoms, foam tablets, and the sponge and salt water technique—
a clinic was opened in the Farah Maternity Hospital. Because
Farah Hospital is located in South Teheran and handles some
40,000 cases annually, it was a logical site for the first clinic and
earliest efforts concentrated on communicating the planned parenthood message through postpartum visits. The Pathfinder Fund
of America offered assistance in the development and operation
of these clinical services.

Since 1966 the Farah Hospital has participated in the International Postpartum Program sponsored by the Population Council. About 60 percent of the women who come in for delivery
show an interest in family planning, althongh only 15 to 20 percent actually return for contraceptive services. As word spreads,
however, women not admitted for delivery come to the hospital
to make use of its family planning services.[11]

Efforts to popularize the concepts of family planning and population control have not been restricted to low-income families,
however. Training courses for medical and paramedical personnel were another immediate need which the FPA met. Doctors
and midwives, for the most part, preferred information on family
planning only when it was requested and limited their advice to
contraceptive methods. The FPA urged them to approach family
planning as something more than birth control and encouraged
them to promote its family welfare aspects in the course of examining and treating patients.

From the beginning, the Family Planning Association and the
Teheran School of Social Work also sought to increase government awareness of the urgency of the problem. Both organizations sought progessive legislation in support of women's rights
and in encouragement of smaller families. Both endeavored to
have population control recognized as a priority requirement in
government planning at all levels. According to a former government official, "There is no doubt that the creation of the Family
Planning Association of Iran, with the help of the Teheran

School of Social Work, has had a very significant effect on family planning in Iran. Over a 15-year period, the Family Planning Association has pushed for family planning and birth control. The push of the government in the Fifth Development Plan owes much to the support of the Shah, the Queen, and government officials for the FPA."[12]

In 1967 the Queen attended the opening of the first community welfare center in Javadieh, an undertaking she had actively supported and for which she had provided funds. At this time, the problems of overcrowding and overpopulation were graphically illustrated to her and she became aware of the pressing need for government sponsorship of a family planning program in order to broaden its reach and give it official sanction. Following her visit, a special division was added to the Ministry of Health to implement the family planning program and an undersecretary was appointed to supervise its activities.

Once the government assumed primary responsibility for the provision of clinical services in 1967, the FPA was able to return to its original goals of social change through educational means. Priority was to be given to education, motivation and follow-up programs, particularly in rural areas and low-income neighborhoods of urban areas. Through family planning, the FPA also wished to lower the rate of induced abortion and resultant complications and to lower the level of infant mortality. In addition, since government clinics were open only in the morning and were thus inaccessible to many working women, the FPA agreed to supplement governmental services until such time as government clinics were open afternoons and evenings.

Family planning activities in Iran have been supported by a number of international organizations. In 1964 the International Planned Parenthood Federation became interested in family planning activities in Iran and invited the chairman of the Family Planning Association of Iran to London to discuss potential assistance from IPPF. She returned to Iran with a British-trained Persian doctor who introduced various contraceptive methods, including the intrauterine device, to other Persian doctors. IPPF has since provided experts and consultants, contraceptive devices (import of the pill was legalized in Iran in 1961 and was supplied by IPPF until government production began in 1967), offered scholarships to its regional and international training programs, and donated such facilities as an equipped mobile unit, teaching models and clinical equipment. The Family Planning Association of Iran is now a member of the IPPF, receiving annual financial assistance.

Assistance is also provided by a United Nations senior population advisor and by the United Nations Fund for Population Activities which has supported a number of projects in Iran. The UN Fund for Population Activities has recently allocated funds to the government of Iran which must go to non-governmental agencies involved in family planning. The FPA has received funds for three projects, one a rural education program described in detail in Chapter VIII, another to provide family life education to youth groups in the communiy welfare centers, and a third to introduce sex education in four high schools in the south of Teheran.

The Population Council has also supported family planning activities in Iran by providing consultants and research grants, donating IUD supplies and subsidizing training both in Iran and abroad. Since 1968, the Population Council has had a resident consultant in Iran.

When the Population Council was invited to send a mission to Iran in 1966, its report also indicated the urgent need for family planning services. On the basis of this report and the advice of other groups including the FPA, the Shah announced in 1970 that the goal for population control would be a one percent annual growth rate to be achieved within 20 years. The goal for the current (Fifth) Development Plan is to reduce the present estimated growth rate of 3.2 percent per year to 2.4 percent, which means that approximately one million births will have to be averted within the next four years.[13]

THE ROLE OF WELFARE PERSONNEL

The need for providing family planning services in Iran was immediately recognized by social work students who were overwhelmed by the tremendous overcrowding found in lower income communities, as discussed in Chapter IX. Women in these communities were usually married by age 15, conceived their first child immediately and had had at least eight pregnancies by the time they were 30. Average life expectancy of women was 35. Because health, education, and welfare facilities were inadequate or unavailable, the children born in these areas were at an immediate disadvantage to other children physically, socially and educationally. Even if services were made available, the social workers and their students felt that unless family size could be reduced, the effectiveness of any social welfare program would be severely limited. And until they had knowledge of family planning methods, parents were denied the opportunity of deciding how many children to have and when to have them.

Since no clinical facilities existed for providing contraceptive devices in 1958, top priority was given to organizing a clinic at Farah Hospital, one of the world's largest maternity hospitals. The initial family planning team at Farah Hospital consisted of a social work student, a doctor, and a midwife. The student social worker's role was to visit women following delivery and talk to them about the advantages of small families over large families. Family planning was approached not as birth control but rather as spacing children so they would arrive when the family actually wanted them and could best care for them. The student tried to explain that by limiting the size of their families, they could contribute to an overall improvement in the family's situation. To emphasize this theme of family improvement, educational films on nutrition, health, hygiene, child care and family planning were shown at the hospital.[14]

Home visits followed postpartum visits. The family planning message was repeated and women were invited to come to the Farah Hospital Clinic (and later to FPA clinics) for medical check-ups and for further family planning information and the provision of contraceptive devices.

Continual home visits are one of the chief means by which social workers have effected attitudinal changes towards family planning in Iran. Large families have long been part of Iranian village tradition, and most of the adults in these poor communities in South Teheran are migrants from rural villages. Because they have grown accustomed to seeing at least half of the children in their villages die, they continue to produce many offspring on the assumption that few will survive. Large families were created quite unexpectedly in the cities, where improved health facilities, in addition to better nutrition and sanitation, lowered infant mortality rates. In rural areas large families, particularly sons, were needed as labor in the fields and as providers in the event of physical disability, or a poor crop. Large families are, of course, almost a universal form of social security for parents in their later years, particularly in rural non-industrialized societies. During the home visits the social workers explained to migrant families that in the cities they no longer need to procreate in anticipation of replacing children, and that rather than improving the family's position by producing many potential breadwinners, they are instead reducing the earning capacities of individual children by forcing them to leave school early to support younger siblings.

Traditional religious attitudes support the concept of large families and folk wisdom has it that good fortune and God's blessing may arrive with the next child. While religion does not appear to be a major obstacle to family planning, many villagers believe that the number of children a family has reflects the will of God and one must submit to His will. When they began to make home visits, students discovered that families who had just arrived in Teheran from rural areas neither questioned the wisdom of having large families nor accepted the most basic responsibilities for them. Going barefoot and wearing rags were accepted by villagers as part of the natural order of things and suggest to urban professionals passive acceptance rather than a belief in active mastery over nature. To counter these attitudes, student social workers armed themselves with passages from the *Koran* on familial responsibilities and the importance of providing one's children with good care and upbringing.

These early home visits proved extremely effective in promoting later visits by the migrant families to the family planning clinic in Farah Hospital. Yet from the beginning it was felt that family planning would only be successful as part of a total welfare effort. While the effect of fewer children on the family's

physical and emotional well-being can clearly be seen, it is equally clear that a cycle exists, that is, an improved family situation in
terms of housing, food, and employment promotes hope for the
future and facilitates the ability to plan. Family planning, in fact,
is frequently *one of the first steps* urban migrants take in attemp-
ting to exert some measure of control over their lives. But people who do not have enough food cannot realistically be expected
to make plans for the future. Because family planning and family
welfare are reciprocally dependent, it is imperative that a family's
immediate needs for food, housing, health, and employment are
met at the same time that a family planning campaign is embark-
ed upon.

It is on this idea that the community welfare centers were
founded. These centers are located in overcrowded, lower income areas in which 80 percent of the heads of households will
typically have been born outside of Teheran. The centers provide family casework, recreational and educational group work
for teenage boys, fathers and mothers, day care for children of
working mothers, and vocational classes for women and teenage
girls. (They are described in detail in Chapter VI.) Each center
also has a Family Planning Association clinic. In the course of
working out other family problems, social workers are able not
only to introduce the concept of family planning, but also to
make immediate referrals to a family planning clinic located in
the same building.

Students at the School of Social Work have field assignments
in both the community welfare centers and the FPA clinics, and
the headquarters of both organizations are on the School's campus, thus tightening the links between the agencies. The student
who introduced family planning to Farah Hospital is now on the
faculty of the School of Social Work where she supervises students doing field work at FPA clinics. Her pioneering program
of intensive home visits has been extended to neighborhoods
around the community welfare centers. Students block off the
neighborhood and, taking two streets at a time, they visit each
house over a two to three month period. Families are acquainted
with the services offered by the centers, including the family
planning clinic. After the women begin to take advantage of the

family planning facilities, follow-up visits are still required to counter their fears and misapprehensions as well as those of their neighbors and relatives. An additional advantage of discussion in the home is that the social worker is able to meet and talk to mothers-in-law and other relatives whose misinformation or negative attitudes towards family planning may dissuade the women from using contraceptives.

Family planning is still approached as part of general family welfare. Women are asked if they feel that they have enough information in areas such as nutrition, child care, health, family relationships, and, of course, family planning. They are also asked if they would be interested in attending classes and, if so, when. These questionnaires are later used by students doing field training in group work when they set up educational programs for women. Women who participate in the family planning programs and in the handicrafts and literacy classes are also invited to attend these educational sessions.

The student invites a physician, midwife, or specialist to address each session on a topic such as population growth, marital relationships and responsibilities, parental health care, infant health and child care, as well as sex problems, family planning and the use of contraceptives. At some centers groups have been formed of mothers who are in the program but still harbor doubts and fears about contraceptives. A doctor or midwife is invited to the clinic to talk to them and answer their questions. Social workers also meet with doctors and midwives at the centers and discuss with them how best to approach the women with the topics of family planning and contraception. Students are responsible for selecting topics, inviting speakers, inviting neighborhood women and, after each session, for holding a discussion to focus on some broad social aspect of the lecture.

While making home visits, the students also recruit young women to act as motivators and thus expand the reach of the family planning program. These girls are given a three to four week training course and are then sent out to continue the home visits. They begin with simple tasks such as informing the mothers of upcoming educational programs or films at the center and follow-up of contraceptive acceptors. If women are unable to visit the clinic, the motivators deliver contraceptive supplies to the home. Dropouts from the family planning program are also followed up by the motivators. If the motivator cannot solve a problem, she informs the student social worker who may then refer the woman to a health clinic or the social welfare department of the center. This followup activity has had notable success in reducing the number of drop-outs in the program.

Later the motivators will help recruit new contraceptive acceptors. Social work students are responsible for supervising motivators. They may go along on home visits to help the motivator improve her method of approaching the client. Every six months, the student social worker evaluates the performance of the motivators. The students are, in turn, supervised by faculty members of the School of Social Work.

The success of home visits can be measured by the number of women visiting the clinics, the drop in the birth rate, and by the lessening of the resistance met by students and motivators.

Koye Nohom Aban, a housing development opened in 1967 in South Teheran, represents one example of a successful family planning motivation program. The majority of the residents are from lower socio-economic classes with the breadwinner usually employed as a manual laborer or a peddler. The population of this community is between 30,000 and 40,000. At the present time, approximately 2,500 women take advantage each year of the family planning services offered by both the FPA and a government clinic.[15] Student social workers and young community residents have made home visits in an attempt to motivate the women to utilize the facilities, and educational programs have been organized at the community welfare center. An expansion of the motivation program has been launched with male social work students working with fathers. A milk distribution program is also used to attract participants. Only women who enroll in the family planning program can receive free milk for their children and the free milk is discontinued if the woman becomes pregnant.

The decline in the birth rate and infant mortality rate attest to the success of the program. The average number of pregnancies per female in the Koye Nohom Aban district dropped from nine in 1967 to 4.5 in 1972. Although a sophisticated cohort analysis or a variety of longitudinal studies are unavailable, there are some data that shed light on the success of the program. For example, the infant mortality rate has decreased from 407 per thousand in 1966, before the center opened, to 154 per thousand in 1967 and, in 1972, was down to 70 per thousand.

One field supervisor for family planning claims that she has more difficulty with student attitudes than with those of the people the students are working with. Most students feel that Iran is underpopulated and requires more trained manpower, particularly for its rapidly developing industry. Some students suspect that family planning is only for the poor and thus represents a measure of social injustice and is possibly promoting institutional bias. It has been necessary to stress at the Teheran School of Social Work that Iran lacks the facilities and services to cope with a rapidly increasing population, and that it is illusory to believe that "the wealth of the poor is in their children." The students are acquainted with the notion that untrained, uneducated children growing up in conditions of poor health and inadequate diet and sanitation are not a source of wealth either to parents or to the society as a whole.

Additional problems with attitudes towards family planning existed, even among field supervisors. To counteract this, a series of seminars by international experts in the field of family planning and population problems was held at the school for faculty and supervisors. Furthermore, all students are now required to take a three-year sequence in population problems, family planning and sex education.

While wives and mothers may well favor smaller families, as KAP studies suggest, they will bow to the wishes of their husbands.[16] One fear harbored by women, and reinforced by their mothers-in-law, is that their husbands will leave them if they fail to conceive annually. The husbands may want women who can demonstrate their own youth and the man's virility by producing a child. Among low-income, illiterate families, the status of a woman in the eyes of her husband and in-laws has traditionally been determined by the number of children, especially sons, which she has. Not only does it go against long-established tradition to ask a woman to make an important decision herself, but, in the case of family planning, the decision being asked of her may erode her only base of security as the mother of many sons.

In the villages, girls were married off when they reached puberty. Their fathers thus no longer had to support them or worry about protecting their virginity. In addition, the father would receive a bridal payment from the groom's family. In the cities, however, minimum marriage age laws are more strictly enforced. Since their fathers saw no reason to educate daughters, they sat at home doing nothing while waiting for someone to find them a husband. For this reason, handicrafts classes as well as literacy classes were organized for them at the community welfare centers.

At the centers girls and young women are encouraged to think about themselves. They are taught grooming, how to dress properly, and how to care for themselves and improve their personal appearance. Physical education classes have recently been organized and are proving extremely popular. Female health problems and the importance of personal hygiene and prenatal care are discussed. Women whose appearance and general health have declined through repeated pregnancies serve as examples to younger women who are encouraged to conclude that by limiting the size of their families they may, in fact, improve their chances for keeping their husbands. They can expect to keep their teeth, their figures, and their general health and strength.

Women and girls are also taught reading and vocational skills at the centers to encourage them to view themselves as something more than childbearers. These new skills, in addition to fostering self-respect, provide them with a means of adding to the family income and demonstrating their economic usefulness when they are not tied down to large families. Young girls are now often capable of earning more than their fathers.

Men also have many doubts and misconceptions about contraceptives, particularly about the pill. They frequently also want more children, although once the child is conceived, the husbands relinquish all responsibility for it to their wives. To change these attitudes, social workers in conjunction with the Family Planning Association have tried to reach both fathers and teenage boys. Fathers Clubs have been set up at the community welfare centers and, among the topics discussed at club meetings are the socio-economic implications of population growth, and, on a more personal level, of large families. Films on marital relationships and responsibilities have been shown at the centers in the evening. Mobile teams have been sent to factories and workshops, especially in the provinces, to inform the workers of planned parenthood programs and available facilities including clinics. However, because of their working hours (many of them hold two jobs) and their lack of interest, it has been difficult to set up educational sessions for men.

Youth are a much more flexible, open and enthusiastic group. Changes in their attitudes will be reflected not only in the coming generations but carry over to their parents who may still be having children. Principals and teachers in schools near the centers have been approached in an attempt to introduce into the high school curriculum problems of population growth and its effect on the economic, environmental, psychological and social welfare of the country.

Experimental efforts have also been made to introduce sex education at the high school level. As indicated earlier, the Family Planning Association has recently received a grant from the United Nations Fund for Population Activities to develop and institute as a pilot project sex education classes in four high schools in South Teheran. The curriculum and teaching materials are being developed by social workers who will also provide classroom instruction.

In another effort to reach adolescents, classes in family life education—also financed by a UNFPA grant—are now being included among the after-school programs for teenage boys in the community welfare centers. Along with providing specific information on sexual changes during puberty, personal hygiene, contraception, recognition and prevention of venereal disease, these classes cover the broader implications of the population explosion, and family roles and responsibilities in an attempt to redirect the traditional attitudes of their fathers. By late 1973, 33 sessions had been held at nine centers and attended by 550 boys. Additional classes for fathers were also held. An indication of the success of the program is that a number of mothers of boys in the program have become contraceptive acceptors in the family planning program. The boys are urged to speak to their mothers, and refer them to the family planning clinics for help and advice. The argument they give is that their own opportunities and those of their siblings will be increased if they are not forced to drop out of school to help support younger children.

Community education also takes place in rural areas where government clinical facilities are available but where people have not been using them sufficiently. Student social workers, sent to rural communities for field work training, find the local leaders whom the people respect and will listen to. Their support is enlisted in motivating the community. Village councils, religious leaders and parent-teacher associations are among the groups who have been involved in family planning efforts in the villages.

Other governmental groups working in the provinces, such as the literacy corps, health corps, and rural development and home economics agents, have also been approached by both the government as well as the social welfare personnel so that they may include family planning in their community development work. However, because most of these workers at the village level are still men, their ability to reach the rural women, especially on a subject such as family planning, is limited. The School of Social Work in conjunction with the Family Planning Association therefore developed a rural population education program (described in Chapter VIII) to train young, female primary or high school graduates to visit women in their own communities and tell them about family planning and the availability of local services. In the process, women are instructed in health, sanitation, and nutrition as well as in family planning. Recently, with the cooperation of the Ministry of Education, literacy instruction has been added to the responsibilities of these young motivators, and family planning may be introduced in the course of teaching women to read and write.

The mass media have been used to reach a larger public. Radio broadcasts have carried family planning messages and articles have appeared in women's magazines. A cinerama unit has been covering villages in the south of Teheran as a pilot project.

One of the most important roles of social welfare personnel is to push for legislation and policies in support of their programs. Among the recent supportive laws and policies which effect family planning efforts are the following, most of which were adopted partially as the result of recommendations from the FPA and the Teheran School of Social Work:

1. The pregnancy and birth allowance may soon be abolished, and consideration is being given to modifying the child allowance law to limit to two the number of children supported.
2. Until recently the minimum legal age for marriage was 16 for girls. In the summer of 1974 the minimum legal age for marriage was raised to 18 for girls and 20 for boys.
3. Divorce now requires court action, and women are obtaining more rights in custody of children after divorce.
4. New family laws affecting the practice of pologamy have been enacted. A man wishing to take a second wife must now obtain the approval of his first wife in addition to court approval, which is given less and less frequently.
5. The Award to the Mother of the Year has in the past been given to the mother of a large family. Now it is given to a mother who has provided the best care and education to a smaller number of children.
6. The Shah has recently announced that military personnel will only receive benefits for up to two children.
7. Contraceptive devices can now be obtained free through any government or FPA clinic.
8. In mid-1973, legislation was adopted legalizing abortion and sterilization.
9. Vasectomy and tubal ligation are now available in some hospitals free of charge.
10. Many maternity hospitals which formerly were free are now charging a fee after the second or third child.

Other social welfare programs and policies fostered by the government will eventually have an effect on population growth. As the role and status of women change, they become more concerned about family planning. Studies made in Iran indicate the close correlation between a high rate of literacy and small family size.[17] Of paramount importance, of course, is the mass illiteracy campaign. In addition, a segment of the country's social welfare manpower is devoted to the improvement of the social situation of women and to the more adequate functioning and expansion of family protection laws. Educational programs in family welfare centers teach child care, family nutrition and health. Vocational classes provide women with new or expanded skills.

Aiso of great importance are new pension and insurance programs which should revise existing attitudes about the need for large families. Iranians have long operated under the assumption that protection against the hardships of old age, unemployment, disability and crop failure can only be obtained through the rearing of a number of children, particularly sons. As the government has introduced pension and insurance programs, the very real economic need to bear and rear a number of children has been reduced. Strong efforts are being made to extend this coverage to the rural population.

THE ROLE OF THE GOVERNMENT

Strong support for the family planning program has come from the Shah who joined 29 other world leaders in 1967 in signing a Declaration on Population which was presented to the United Nations Secretary General U Thant. As stated earlier, in 1970, the Shah stated that the goal of population control would be a one percent annual growth rate, to be achieved over the next 20 years.

Family planning is seen as contributing to the overall economic welfare of the country. Among its benefits will be a better ratio between youth and adults and the subsequent increase in the percentage o fthe population who are contributing to the economy, producing rather than simply consuming. With a high birth rate, the median age of the population steadily decreases and the number of economically dependent members of society keeps on rising. From 1956 to 1966, the population under age 15 increased from 42 to 46 percent. A decline in infant mortality also contributed to this increase. The youth dependency ratio (population aged 0–14 divided by population aged 15-64) of .77 in 1956 increased to .92 in 1966 (as compared with a youth dependency ratio of 65.8 in 1966 in the United States).[18] The effect of population growth on economic growth was expressed by the Shah in the following statement:

Iran has fortunately now reached the stage of economic take-off. Developing countries producing raw materials are as a rule backward and have very high rates of population growth. We usually find that countries without proper recreational activities have high rates of population growth, and that while the population of such countries is increasing at annual rates of 3 or 3:5 percent, their economic growth is nil or a minus quantity. The reason for this is that the prices of the raw materials they export drop year by year at the whim of the consumer countries, because the consumers are really the purchasers, and can dictate their own prices while steadily increasing the prices of the products they sell themselves. So the backward or developing countries grow steadily poorer while their populations rise, the prices of the raw materials they export drop and the prices at which they have to purchase their requiremenst rise. This state of affairs cannot continue.[19]

In 1967 family planning became the responsibility of the Ministry of Health and an undersecretary for family planning was appointed to the Ministry to implement the program. The Plan and Budget Organization provides the Ministry with the greatest share of its budget, and its contribution to family planning has increased from U.S. $600,000 in 1968-1969 to about $5.4 million in 1971-1972. Friesen estimates that actual expenditures on family planning are between $10 and $12 million, with the difference being expended by other agencies.[20]

The broad, long-term objectives of the national family planning program as stated by the Ministry of Health are:
1. To secure the physical, mental, social and economic welfare of the society through the welfare of the family.
2. To reduce induced abortion and its complications.
3. To coordinate the population growth rate and income per capita.
4. To balance the age structure of the population.
5. To increase the percentage of the economically active population.

The plan of action includes attention to education, the establishment of family planning clinics, the development of policies in program administration and various demographic measurements, evaluation and research.

EDUCATION

Education sessions have been held for farmers, office workers, laborers and parent-teacher associations in all provinces. Efforts have been made to reach the armed forces, police force and gendarmerie, as well as religious leaders and various professional groups. Mass media have been used to draw public attention to the social and economic implications of family planning. Population and family planning are among the topics under discussion at the annual medical congresses.

Family planning teaching is incorporated in the work of the revolutionary corps, including the literacy, health, and extension and development corps. Corps members who are sent to the rural areas to help improve the standard of living also promote family planning. The health corps distributes contraceptives via mobile units. In addition, the women's health corps plays an important role in distributing family planning information and services.[21]

ESTABLISHMENT OF FAMILY PLANNING CLINICS

Family planning units have been set up in health centers, maternal and child health centers, and maternity homes and hospitals. Since mothers are reluctant to attend isolated family planning clinics, family planning units have been placed in existing medical facilities. By mid-1971, 1,529 clinics were offering family planning services, 678 run by the Ministry of Health and 851 by other organizations. Most of these were in urban areas and few were limited strictly to the provision of contraceptive services. Of the contraceptive methods offered by these clinics, the pill is by far the most widely accepted.[22]

In principle, a medical team of a doctor, midwife, assistant nurse and other paramedical personnel are responsible for a family planning unit. However, there is a serious shortage of medical and paramedical personnel in Iran. In 1971 there were only 337 gynecologists, of whom 219 were in Teheran; 90.4 percent of midwives and 92.3 percent of graduate nurses are in urban areas. The predominantly rural provinces of the country, with a population of over ten million people, have 142 midwives, 25 gynecologists and 234 graduate nurses.[23] To reach the two-thirds of the country's population living in villages, mobile teams have been set up. These 37 government mobile teams operating in rural areas promote public health and raise standards of hygiene in addition to promoting family planning.

DEVELOPMENT OF POLICIES

Population policies are being developed on the basis of demographic research. A council is responsible for studying food, education and housing resources, rural development, and the social and economic resources of the country in order to develop appropriate population policies.

DEMOGRAPHIC MEASUREMENTS, EVALUATION AND RESEARCH

Recent research includes census analyses, studies of birth rates among different socio-economic groups, KAP, studies of the effectiveness of different communication methods in reaching the public, studies of abortion and miscarriage, studies of the effectiveness of different contraceptive methods as well as evaluations of family planning services and the activities of clinics run by the Ministry of Health and other agencies.

MANPOWER AND TRAINING

Necessary to any national family planning program is an adequate supply of trained personnel: medical, paramedical, social welfare, administrators, and other professional staff. These people are involved in motivation, public education and communication.[24] A recent inventory indicates that there are approximately 50,000 agents in Iran who are directly or indirectly involved in family planning communication and motivation. These agents include the members of the development, health and literacy corps and home economics extension agents, as well as trained social workers, mostly in urban areas, and less trained social welfare per-workers, mostly in urban areas, and less formally trained social welfare personnel, mostly in rural areas.[25]

The Ministry of Health with 1,746 agents has the largest staff directly involved in family planning (communication and motivation). These included, in 1970, 304 assistant social workers, 21 social workers, 283 family planning agents and 1,138 women's health corps members.[26] By 1973, 38 social workers were employed in the family planning programs of the Ministry of Health.

In addition to medical, paramedical and social welfare personnel and revolutionary corps members, many others are involved indirectly with family planning, including personnel associated with local community social organizations such as village councils, rural justice and cultural houses, and health committees.

Because of the shortage of higher level professional staff, the government plans to increase the number of paramedical personnel in villages and to delegate the less demanding tasks to the lowest possible staff level.[27] In addition to the shortage of doctors and nurses, particularly in rural areas, there is a shortage of social workers. The country's only social work school, the Teheran School of Social Work, has increased from 20 students in 1958 to 336 in 1974-1975. There are presently about 50 social workers involved with family planning motivation and another 50 involved with the provision of direct services. In addition, approximately 500 assistant social workers (with from six months' to two years' training) are involved in family planning activities.

The Family Planning Division of the Ministry of Health operates a number of training centers of which the oldest and largest is the Firouzgar Center in Teheran. In addition to short training courses in the provinces, it offers various intensive training courses for many of the medical, paramedical and field personnel who will be active in providing family planning services.[28]

The Family Planning Division reported during 1970–1971 that approximately 57,400 individuals participated in various family planning short courses offered in different provinces of Iran.[29] By mid-1971, over 40,000 male recruits to the literacy corps had received family planning training, as well as more than 5,000 members of the extension and development corps, 500 home economics agents, 1,000 cooperative society supervisors, and 500 volunteers of the Women's Organization. By mid-171, there were seven training centers for rural midwives and additional programs have since been established.

Formal courses in family planning are offered in universities, specialized institutions of higher education, and public and private high schools. Socio-demographic courses are offered at Teheran University, National University in Teheran, Pahlavi University in Shiraz and the University of Isfahan, and at least 61 faculty members are involved in the population field. In addition, the School of Public Health at Teheran University offers a Master's degree with a specialization in family planning. Courses in family planning and related subjects are also offered in the School of Social Work, the 11 schools of nursing and 41 schools of *Behyari* (assistant nurses). The Ministry of Education has introduced population education material into junior and senior high school curricula to acquaint young people with the perils of population growth and the importance of family planning.[30]

Student social worker making a home visit for community survey.

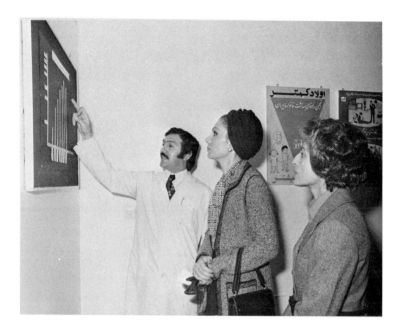

A gynecologist explains a family planning acceptance chart.

The Teheran School of Social Work.

Family Planning Education in an FPA clinic.

The Queen visits an after-school art class for teen-agers.

The Queen visits an after-school youth activity group.

A group of women explain their problems to the Empress.

The Queen visits a literacy class for women.

The Queen visits a knitting class for young women.

An evening adult education program in a Community Welfare Center.

VI   Community Welfare Centers

The primary goals of the White Revolution are to help people attain a higher level of living and a high degree of social justice. The community welfare centers, which offer programs to help people improve their life situation and to work toward social and economic progress and independence, are a direct outgrowth of these goals.

Background of the Community Welfare Center Movement

In 1962 an unusually severe spring flood left many people homeless in Javadieh, a suburb in southwest Teheran composed primarily of low-income workers who had recently migrated to the city from rural areas. Students from the School of Social Work, at the request of government officials, were immediately dispatched to Javadieh to help with flood relief. In addition, people in the Teheran community contributed funds and volunteered their services to help with temporary programs for child care, feeding and shelter in tents until permanent plans could be made.

On the basis of a field study conducted by faculty and students of the School, provision of day care facilities for children without families or whose families were unable to care for them was defined as a particularly pressing need during the period of resettlement. A garden day care program accommodating 200 children was quickly established by the School.

Following resettlement, a review of family situations clarified the need for continued day care services. Many mothers were compelled to work to support their families, either because the father's income was inadequate or because he was dead or absent. After a search for suitable space, a prominent Teheran citizen donated a building rent-free and the permanent day care program was reduced to 60 children with a staff of three teachers, a cook and supportive personnel including student social workers. The entire project was under the supervision of the faculty of the Teheran School of Social Work.

It soon became clear, however, that children were not the only ones in need of help. Most of the families had recently migrated from villages and retained their village traditions while faced with many urban problems. The men, who had previously been farmers, were totally unequipped for urban employment. Few were literate. Housing was in scarce supply and as people poured into the city, frequently following severe winters and subsequent food shortages in the rural areas, shanty towns sprang up which served as transit camps. Large families were crammed into primitive quarters lacking sanitation, ventilation and all but the meagerest of furnishings. Most of the women, in addition to being illiterate, lacked any knowledge of sanitation, hygiene or proper diet. Since their husbands, lacking education and skills, were often unable to provide for their families, many women were forced into employment, thus leaving the families further uncared for. Obviously, the reduction of poverty and the improvement of living conditions for the community as a whole were essential.

Gradually, a cluster of services was seen to be needed and the concept of community welfare centers evolved step by step. When the critical need for services was reported to Queen Farah, she contributed 2,000,000 rials (approximately $26,500) toward the construction and equipment of a new, larger, and better-staffed community center to replace the inadequate donated space. The new center would be able to provide a range of services in addition to day care. Immediately after the Queen's gift, the students were organized into a fund-raising group to obtain money, land and materials. Individual students contacted construction companies and obtained bricks, tile, cement and other materials. Other students saw merchants and obtained donations of curtains, food, furniture, refrigerators, kitchen equipment and other equipment and supplies. The Mayor of Teheran gave 2,060 square meters of land for the building site. Additional contributions came from charitable persons and groups and, in the summer of 1966, the School of Social Work contracted for the construction of the building. The new center opened for service on October 26, 1966.

SERVICES OFFERED BY THE COMMUNITY WELFARE CENTER

1. Day Care.

Day care service for children has served as the nucleus of the community welfare center program since the beginning, both because it is a primary requirement in areas where so many women are required to work and because it initially attracts the greatest number of women to the center. Once the women have been introduced to the community welfare center through day care for their children, they become acquainted with the rest of the program. While they are observing the care the child receives at the center, attempts are made to upgrade the care the child will receive at home. Next, programs in hygiene, sanitation, nutrition, health and family planning are introduced. Once the women begin to acquire the practical information which they are anxious to have, their educational diet is supplemented with literacy and vocational classes. When the mothers are active in the programs offered by the center, they are encouraged to enroll their older children in the youth programs. Thus, the day care center, which began initially with the woman who had to work, has been redesigned to train, encourage and emancipate the woman who wants to work. With increased industrialization in Iran, more and more mothers are employed and day care is emerging as a paramount requirement.

In addition to providing recreation, health care and improved diet for the children, the day care program is designed to aid their social development as individuals and as members of their peer groups, families and communities.

Thirteen of the eighteen community welfare centers in operation in early 1973 had day care services available to the children of working mothers living in the community, with preference given to the children of working mothers who cannot adequately care for children economically, socially and psychologically. Most of the centers with day care programs hope to expand their facilities to serve the communities more adequately. And most of those centers without programs consider as a priority need the acquisition of a larger building to house a day care program.

2. Family planning, maternal and child health.

With the objective of developing a healthier new generation, the community welfare centers have enlisted the aid of gynecologists, social workers, nurses, midwives and other paramedical personnel. For example, the incidence of contagious disease is still very high in Iran and constitutes one of the major health problems of the country, as a review of the state of public health indicates.* The centers are approaching the problem of contagious diseases by teaching sanitation and cleanliness, by making referrals to appropriate treatment facilities, and by arranging annual vaccinations and other preventive measures.

A primary target of health work at the center is prenatal care. If the mother is healthy and receives proper care and nutrition during pregnancy, the chances that her child will be healthy are greatly improved. Pregnant women are cared for and steps have been taken to lower infant mortality. Additional health programs include the treatment of gynecological problems, testing for cervical cancer, provision of medical examinations and health cards for employees of the centers, overall preventive measures, and referrals to hospitals and other facilities.

All the community welfare centers have family planning clinics run by the Family Planning Association of Iran, or they are currently working toward them. Following medical examinations, women are given the birth control devices they prefer or require, free of charge. Education is the core of the family planning effort and the advantages of small families, for which the

---

*For example, contagious diseases per thousand of the population in 1967 included: dysentery 26; influenza 21.7; conjunctivitis 9.5; measles 4.3; trachoma 4.2; malaria 2.5; whooping cough 2.2; mumps 2.2; and pulmonary tuberculosis 1.1.

best care and opportunities can be provided, are explained to the women through home visits as well as in small gatherings with films, slides, and discussions.

3. Literacy.

Following one of the most important principles of the White Revolution, about half the community welfare centers have organized literacy classes to teach mothers and other adult members of the family to read and write. (In areas where the government's literacy corps is active, classes have not been organized in the community welfare center.) One of the primary advantages of these literacy classes is in broadening the general understanding of the women of the community and opening new horizons of a cultural and intellectual nature.

4. Handicrafts.

Because many women have to work to augment the very small earnings of unskilled laborers with large families in the poor sections of urban areas, and since most of the women are also unskilled, handicrafts classes have been inaugurated to provide these women with skills. Regular classes are held for the instruction of sewing, knitting and weaving (including rugs) to the mothers and young girls. In addition to providing them with marketable skills, these classes contribute to the development of homemaking abilities.

The classes are designed according to the requirements of the local community, the interests of the women in the community, availability of materials, and the marketability of the finished products. Thus, handicraft programs differ in Teheran and the provinces and an effort is made to teach the women something that could benefit them economically in the place in which they are living. Handicrafts made in the program are often sold and savings accounts are opened for the women and girls to enable them to buy the necessary equipment in order to continue their vocations independently when they complete the courses. The centers evaluate the progress of the students and help them enter the job market. A sewing diploma, received after six months, entitles its holder to apply for work as a sewing instructor in one of the centers or to work in industry or at home. Social workers maintain contact with the women not only through the classes, but afterwards, in order to encourage them and enable them to receive the most from the welfare centers.

5. Youth programs.

One of the major activities of the centers is the planning and development of multipurpose youth programs. After-school and summer programs include educational, social and recreational components for teenagers and are consciously designed to reinforce and strengthen their classroom studies. With the support of government ministries, educational films are shown, lectures are presented, musical programs and art exhibitions are planned, and opportunities are available for sports, drama, music, hobbies, and the development of skills. At one center, 85 boys between the ages of 12-18 study painting, theatre, newspaper work, and photography. Sports include football, volleyball, chess, and ping pong.

The stress on youth programs stems from the conviction that this group is particularly vulnerable as well as malleable, and requires self-knowledge, practice in making decisions independently and the development of social skills. Moreover, from this group will come the future generation of craftsmen, professionals, and leaders.

Many young boys in crowded, low-income areas have little to do and lack any recreational facilities to keep them occupied. Surrounded by unfavorable social and economic pressures, they can easily become delinquent. Much of their free time is spent in teahouses or on street corners. Drug abuse, theft, and other delinquencies are common in their neighborhoods. The youth programs aim not only at preventing deviant behavior in young men and boys, but also at providing them with self-confidence and self-knowledge and at preparing them to accept the heavy responsibilities that await them.

6. *Adult Education.*

Each center plans fathers' clubs and adult group discussions for the evenings after the youth activities have ended. Adults, particularly fathers, are made acquainted with national developments and are taught principles of civic responsibility and skills of community betterment. In addition, some programs are designed to improve vocational skills and other programs to promote family planning.

7. *Social service department.*

Each center has a social welfare department and most of the twenty-two centers have at least one social worker. Social work services are critically needed for a variety of reasons. Many families need help in locating employment. Laborers need advice and counsel in taking advantage of the government's Labor Social Insurance which is available, but unfamiliar, to them. Some families need emotional support in times of crisis, as well as help in solving day-to-day problems with their in-laws and relatives, caring for their children and avoiding unwanted pregnancies. Social workers are often able to refer clients to other services offered by the center. For example, financial crises can be handled by the Family Aid Society which helped 1,570 people during 1971 at a cost of 360,000 rials ($4,800).

It is considered so important for the social worker to have at least some direct contact with families in the community that a special corps of social work students was assigned to visit and talk with every other family, house by house, in Koye Nohom Aban Community Center which services a low-income population. Even though all families will not take immediate advantage of the services of the community welfare center, it is highly desirable that families know where to turn if and when they are in need.

The only graduate social worker on the staff is generally the center director. All centers now have directors who are graduate social workers. One or two field work supervisors are in charge of the social work department at each center, supervising both second and third year students. Students spend an entire school year at one center, giving them time to become acquainted with the community. Third year students also remain through much of the summer.

A social work student interviews and visits the home of any family using the center. Recommendations are made, on the basis of the interviews and home visits, as to admission to the center's programs, since demand far exceeds available space.

Second year students devote themselves exclusively to casework, with children from the day care program, and their parents, youth in the after-school program and their parents, cases referred from the family planning clinic with problems other than those of birth control (a separate social worker is assigned to the family planning clinic to deal specifically with problems diectly related to family planning), and cases who are referred from outside to the center. Generally, they are faced with family problems: a youth who feels neglected since a sibling is favored over him; children of divorced or separated parents, when one parent is creating problems. The students also arrange meetings with the mothers of children in the day to interpret the different services at the center. Third year students, in addition to casework, are involved in group work services to youth and parents, and in community work.

The group work programs include educational programs for mothers and fathers. The fathers' programs are the most difficult and the fewest in number, since the men complain of lack of time and lack of interest. The mothers and the boys are much more eager. Educational programs are set up for the mothers on the fundamentals of nutrition, hygiene, health, family planning, child care, and marital relationships.

The second semester of the third year, students work in community organization. Generally, they carry out one project, focusing on the particular need of the community: water, electricity, building new roads or paving existing ones, improving sewage and sanitation, enriching and expanding mass education. The students go about finding out the specific needs of a particular community in various ways. They have already had a semester of work in the community and have gotten to know residents. They talk to community leaders, work through the schools, call meetings, or may simply engage a group of people in the street in conversation. Then they work with the people and the relevant community or government officials to help bring about the desired change or improvement. Communities are taught how to get together, focus on a particular problem, and go about solving it.

A successful program was sponsored by the social work department in the Koye Nohom Aban Center for one week in the summer of 1972 in an all-out effort to change existing community attitudes and to stimulate the people to improve their situation. The previous month had been devoted to publicizing the effort. Tents were set up outdoors and were manned by social work, medical and paramedical personnel. The role of the social worker was explained, job counseling was offered, dieticians and mental health workers discussed their work, school personnel were available to discuss school problems, and family planning personnel promoted birth and population control. An x-ray unit was available and chest problems spotted during the week were followed up afterwards. Eye examinations were given. A dentist was available; dental hygiene was explained and toothbrushes and toothpaste were distributed. Medicine and some foods which had been donated were passed out. Various audio-visual devices were also used to explain and inform. The educational process was two-way: professionals learned about community problems and how to deal with them and the neighborhood residents were made aware of the services available to them, primarily those offered by the community welfare center.

An additional application of social work skill is in encouraging the government to use the example of the community welfare centers to reach into every corner of the country. The Teheran School of Social Work has revised its curriculum to include more teaching of social policy and legislation in order that future graduates will be able to think more broadly and comprehensively and to carry out programs of social action and reform as well as to influence the government to implement broader programs of social development.

8. *In-service training for paraprofessionals and volunteers.*

Each center, in cooperation with the Teheran School of Social Work, carries on a training program to instruct and educate teachers to work with pre-school children. Such a program has the multiple advantages of opening up new career opportunities for women, while at the same time enriching the day care center curriculum and expanding the knowledge and skills base of mothers.

In addition, neighborhood women are trained as motivators in the family planning program and visit community women in their homes to inform them of the importance of family planning and the availability of facilities. Training in the vocational and handicraft programs enables some of the graduates to become instructors in the program. Women are also trained to assist social workers and midwives and to provide cleaning help.

DEVELOPMENT OF ADDITIONAL CENTERS

When Queen Farah visited the new Javadieh Center on November 3, 1966, she expressed her financial and moral commitment to the establishment of similar community welfare centers as they were requested by people in other needy areas in the south of Teheran, the area bearing the brunt of rural emigration. Accordingly, faculty and students of the School of Social Work surveyed the slums of South Teheran and found that a priority need existed in the Park Valiahd area. The project was developed and students were again organized to raise funds and supplies. The Municipality of Teheran donated 7,500 square meters of park land for a site. Funds for construction were contributed by the Queen and other interested parties, including the Siemens Corporation of Germany. In October 1967 this center began providing service to needy children and their families.

The School also secured 3,000 square meters of land from the Voosough family in the densely populated, low-income southeast district. The Queen again donated funds for a building and in September 1969, the Solaymanieh Community Welfare Center opened.

Meanwhile, the need for community welfare centers in the provinces outside Teheran had been recognized. As early as the summer of 1964, the School of Social Work had been asked to survey community needs in the city of Yazd, a desert town in central Iran which is the main stronghold of the ancient Zoroastrian community. Industrialization in Yazd had impoverished workers in the handloom industry, for which the town has long been famous. As a result of the survey, the Yazd Foundation was established with a volunteer membership interested in the betterment of the people of Yazd. The School and Foundation worked together to organize a community welfare center for the children of workers in the handloom industry.

Once they saw how the centers stimulated economic improvement in family situations, families from other areas began to demand services. Often the community would request a study of its needs. Students from the School of Social Work were sent to these communities to survey their particular needs and on the basis of the surveys, new centers were planned. Thus not all community welfare centers are the same. Two centers which offor very specialized services are the red light district, where social workers work with prostitutes on such matters as contraception, hygiene, health and child care, and the Darvaze Ghar[1] area, an extremely poor community whose residents live in abandoned sites, including kilns and burrows in the ground. Here, problems of addiction and delinquency are especially prevalent.

The School of Social Work took responsibility for extending these centers in Teheran and other cities. The original community welfare centers had proved so successful that the Ministry of Labor, which had created four centers to handle social service programs for workers and their families, gave these centers to the Community Welfare Center of Iran to operate.

With the increasing number of centers and their recognized effectiveness, it became clear that an independent governing body, other than the Teheran School of Social Work, was necessary. After an overall plan was developed, a central body was established to oversee the welfare centers. On May 19, 1970, the Community Welfare Center of Iran was approved, registered and inaugurated.

By January 1974, a total of 22 community welfare centers had been established, including a specialized welfare center for prostitutes in Teheran. Others are being developed. Including Javadieh, Park Valiahd, Solaymanieh and Yazd, the 22 centers currently in operation include thirteen in Teheran and nine in the provinces. The government, on the basis of the successful pilot project, has committed itself to build 100 community welfare centers in priority areas and has allocated funds for this purpose.[2]

OBJECTIVES OF THE COMMUNITY WELFARE CENTER OF IRAN

The Community Welfare Center was established to raise the economic standards and improve the social and cultural conditions of low-income families throughout the country by fulfilling their needs through the self-help method. This objective is achieved by the following means:

1. By helping people to participate in the physical betterment of their environment, to instill in them a sense of community responsibility.

2. By improving educational standards, to promote and facilitate upward mobility.

3. By developing local communities (including identifying and educating local leaders), to help the people administer their own affairs.

4. By carrying out research studies on institutions rendering welfare services, to improve the coordination of these services as well as to reach a better understanding of actual social needs.

5. By providing educational and training programs, to enable youth to understand and cope with future technology, thereby contributing to the reduction of poverty and illiteracy.

6. By providing day care facilities and vocational programs, to encourage and enable mothers to work and thereby raise the economic level of their families.

THE RELEVANCE OF THE COMMUNITY WELFARE CENTER
MOVEMENT TO THE OBJECTIVES OF THE WHITE REVOLUTION.

The community welfare center is an example of a residual approach to social welfare as opposed to a developmental or institutional approach, in that it provides services primarily to the low-income families in overcrowded and underdeveloped urban areas.[3]

However, there are developmental aspects of the community welfare center, since the objective is to serve entire low-income neighborhoods without any clearcut needs test or other device for excluding families. As in all industrializing countries, Iran has developed a system of so-called residual services while the institutional or developmental services such as the social insurances and universal health care are being implemented. The goal of the new Ministry of Social Welfare is to provide universal social insurance and universal medical care, and it is expected that these programs will be fully in operation within the next five to ten years.

The residual sevices, nevertheless, will continue to be important as long as large numbers of rural families continue to move into the larger cities, presenting a complex number of interlocking needs such as for vocational training, adult education, home-making skills, and social services. These families will require specific programs designed for their unique situation. The community welfare center movement is such a program.

The community welfare center movement fits directly into the social justice and economic redistribution objectives of the White Revolution. Underprivileged families are being provided with resources and programs aimed at helping them to compensate for inadequacies of education, health, vocational training, recreation, and other services. The ultimate aim of the community welfare movement is to give these rural migrants the same conditions of social justice and access to opportunities as the White Revolution projects for the Iranian population as a whole.

HOW A COMMUNITY IS STUDIED

Since the main purpose for developing community welfare centers is to reduce poverty and to allow the low-income family to reach a higher level of living, it is necessary to examine the nature of this poverty and the conditions of these families, neighborhood by neighborhood. When the School wants to survey an area, the students plan and carry it out with the help of the research faculty. The community of Solaymanieh has been selected as typical. Before a community welfare center was constructed in Solaymanieh, social workers and social work students conducted a census of the area in 1967 to determine the needs of the community. Some of the results of this census are reported below.

1. Demographic make-up of the community.

The community was extremely young, with more than half its population (53 percent) under age 16 and two-thirds under age 25. In general, men marry by age 34, women marry by age 29. Women are frequently married at age 15 or less and men as early as age 16. Of the married women in the community, more than half had already had between two and five pregnancies, with the largest category (15.5%) being three pregnancies. (Unfortunately, comparative data on age at marriage and pregnancy rates are not available from other communities.) The maximum number of pregnancies recorded was 18.

Most of the adults in the community came from rural areas. Of heads of households, only 18 percent were born in Teheran, although most migrated within the Central Province of which Teheran is the capital. Fifty-one percent of the population have lived in Teheran ten years or less, while only 13 percent have lived in Teheran more than 20 years.

The rate of child mortality, 5 per 1,000, was extremely high, with 58 percent of the deaths having occurred in the first year and 92 percent having occurred before age six. Deaths following delivery ran as high as 23 percent, while 6.5 percent of pregnancies ended in miscarriage, and the chances of miscarriage and stillbirth increased with the number of pregnancies. Malnutrition and premature birth were the main causes of death in children less than one year of age and accounted for 26 percent of the deaths. Infectious diseases accounted for 21 percent and lung diseases for another 14 percent. More boys were born than girls and more boys died than girls.

∅ 2. Occupations.

More than three-quarters of the population of Solaymanieh was economically inactive. Children comprised almost one-third of the community, unemployed housewives one-quarter and students one-fifth. Of the 23 percent of the community who were employed, the overwhelming majority were peddlers. Fifty-eight perecnt of the population earned between one and 30 rials per day and only fifteen percent earned more than 50 rials daily.

3. Housing.

Of the 788 households studied, 83 percent lived in private houses for which almost all (95 percent) made monthly payments. More than half of these monthly payments were less than 1,000 rials a month ($13) and only 12 percent paid more than 2,000 rials ($26). Only 14 percent rented their living quarters and the great majority of these rented only a room.

Eighty-six percent of the households lived in one or two rooms. In terms of actual space, three-quarters of the population lived in areas between 11 and 30 square meters in size. Most of the houses, whether private or rented, occupied 30 to 80 square meters, including the yard, and most were not professionally built. Only fifteen percent had three rooms, five percent had four rooms, and less than one percent had five rooms or more.

4. Education and literacy

The educational level in Solaymanieh was very low. Only five percent could read and write; 44 percent of the people over age six were completely illiterate; 34 percent had gone to evening classes or had one to four years of schooling. Only two-tenths of one percent had finished high school. Women had a higher rate of illiteracy than men (55 percent vs 34 percent). Among 441 illiterate men between the ages of 6 and 44, 51 percent said they were willing to attend literacy classes. A smaller number, 47 percent, of

674 illiterate women reported a willingness to learn to read and write.

The largest percentage of students were attending first grade (22 percent) and the percentage decreased every year thereafter, so that only seven percent of all students were in the sixth grade, one percent in the ninth grade and .13 percent in senior high. Also, .13 percent were engaged in higher education.

The preceding material was utilized in designing Solaymanieh Community Welfare Center which opened in 1968.

A VISIT TO A SPECIFIC COMMUNITY WELFARE CENTER IN FALL 1972[4]

The above review of the history, objectives and programs of the Community Welfare Center presents a less than vital picture. The following description of a particular center on a typical day is intended to provide a more vivid account.

Naziabad Center is located, like other Teheran centers, in the south of the city. Unlike other Teheran centers, it is surrounded by high-rise, middle-income apartment buildings whose residents are better educated and financially more secure than most clients of a community welfare center. The building itself, a one-story stone structure, is surrounded by handsomely landscaped gardens and a well-equipped playground. The center is just one year old and the building and land were donated by Bank Rahni of Iran. The interior is light and airy, with plants spread throughout. Careful attention has obviously been paid to furnishing and decoration. The visitor is struck immediately by the paintings on the wall, donated by students at Teheran University. One area is devoted to goldfish and another to birds, and the director was on the lookout for monkeys in the hope of starting a zoo for the children.

The children in the day care classes appeared happy and outgoing, and all the children in one class of four-year olds came up to shake hands with the visitors and welcome them to their class without prompting from the teacher. The programs in the day care classes are imaginative and the children are given free time to work on their own projects. Each week a topic is chosen for all to discuss. The topic during the week of the visit was a study of different animals, and the previous week had been devoted to discussion of mothers. The children make presents for their parents. Parents are encouraged to visit, and a father came to his son's classroom during the morning of the visit. Unfortunately, there is insufficient room for day care classes. Enrollment has been limited to 170 and a great many more children are on a waiting list. The director of the center estimated that, to meet neighborhood needs, the center should have day care facilities for 1,000 children. There are two teachers and one maid for each of the ten classes.

About one hundred boys between the ages of 12 and 18 participate in an after-school youth program from 5 to 8 p.m. Not everyone is accepted for the program and a part-time social worker is available to handle problems. Those in the program pay a nominal monthly fee of 20 rials (26 cents) and are then free to choose two of the programs offered. These include a photography class, which the boys themselves voted into the program, and an English class, both taught by Peace Corps workers, as well as programs on theatre, newspaper work, chess and discussion groups. These groups are run by third-year student social workers who have invited theatre and journalism students from the University of Teheran to work with the boys in producing plays and a handwritten newspaper. The discussion group includes visits to social agencies in Teheran to find out what they do and how they operate. One trip, which interested the boys, was to an orphanage.

Sports facilities are lacking, although a nearby playing field is available for football, and matches with other community welfare centers are arranged by the student social workers. Other sports include chess, ping pong and various table games.

Three second-year students from the Teheran School of Social Work do casework at Naziabad Center as part of their field work, under the supervision of a faculty member at the School. Three third-year social work students do group work, which includes organizing the above programs. In addition to the six unpaid social work students, there is a part-time paid social worker heading up the youth program and a fourth-year social work student who is also paid for the work he does. However, there is no full-time social worker, a serious deficiency in the opinion of the center's director.

The students may call parents to the center to discuss specific problems of their children or may meet with groups of parents to discuss the problems they have in relating to their children, frequently having to do with the parents' failure to listen to their children. Third-year social work students also work in the Naziabad Center in the summer to learn about environmental problems such as health and sanitation. Families come to them with specific complaints, such as the inability to get a telephone installed or dissatisfaction with clinic services. The students then bring these families together with the relevant employees of the telephone company or clinic so that the problems may be discussed directly, solutions arrived at, and previous difficulties, generally in communication, ironed out with a mediating party present.

Classes for girls and women include sewing, knitting and artificial flower-making. In each of these classes, a diploma is awarded after a three to six-month period of study and graduates are helped to secure well-paying jobs.

A well-equipped family planning unit is staffed by a full-time midwife and two part-time doctors, one three mornings a week and the other three afternoons a week.

The building houses a very good, large auditorium where classes and programs are held, including movies, lectures and discussions on child care, family planning, health, nutrition and a variety of subjects of interest to youth, mothers and families. A library contains books in both Persian and English and a magazine rack is filled with the latest issues of magazines for youth.

Other facilities include a bathroom for the maids so they are able to bathe before they begin work in the morning and a laundry room in which staff can launder their uniforms.

The director of the center is a graduate of San Diego State University and holds a Bachelor's degree in Human Services. She has been the only director since the center opened a year ago and has been unusually dedicated to her work.

Inadequacies and problems exist, however, at Naziabad. The day care center does not have enough space to meet community demand for its services. The family planning unit needs a full-time social worker, as does the center itself. Employees have transportation problems in getting to and from work. Children cannot take enough field trips due to lack of transportation. Salaries are too low for many staff categories and employees lack an adequate retirement system.[5]

The visitor is forced to conclude that, in spite of a fresh, vital and creative program administered by an enthusiastic and inspired director, a great deal more support is necessary to keep Naziabad growing and responding to community needs. The government must provide far greater support to the community welfare center movement if it is to realize its full potential.

A Summary of Needs and Problems

The fantastic growth rate of the city of Teheran, presently estimated at seven percent per year, means that whatever is planned is likely to be inadequate by the time it is finished, and, in fact, six centers list lack of space as one of their prime problems. The directors of the nine Teheran centers were recently asked to enumerate their major requirements, and, in addition to more space, transportation to the center ranks high on all lists. Other requests include movie projectors and films, a music teacher, an English teacher, a painting teacher, social workers, improved youth programs, a stage and workshop and a better telephone system. Full-time social workers are in short supply in Iran, and the need is largely met by student social workers. These needs can be summarized as space, staff, transportation and facilities, all requiring a greater level of financial support.

VII Other Social Services
in Urban Areas

Like any urbanizing and industrializing nation, Iran has had to face the need for social services to compensate for the changes forced on the family and other social institutions. The following discussion does not attempt to review all the social services that are being developed. Only those in which the Teheran School of Social Work has played a significant role and in which graduates of the School are employed have been selected. However, the omission of other services should not be interpreted as a reflection on their importance or value.

The Teheran School of Social Work opened its doors to students in 1958 at a time when social services in Iran were rudimentary in development and chaotic in organization. Several areas of social work practice are discussed to highlight the ways in which the new School tried to aid the social development of the country.

CHILD WELFARE
1. Services to dependent and neglected children.

The students in the first years reported, for example, that the orphanage at Aminabad outside Teheran had thousands of children—blind, deaf and dumb, and retarded—housed together with beggars and prostitutes. A 15-year old blind girl had become pregnant while in the orphanage. Serious overcrowding was a problem in addition to poor dietary conditions, sanitation and housing facilities. Treatment was virtually non-existent.

Faculty members of the Teheran School of Social Work accompanied the Mayor of Teheran, Mr. Musa Mohan, in making an unannounced visit to the Aminabad center in 1958. On seeing destitute and uncared-for children covering the floors of the center, the Mayor was shocked and asked for the carefully developed recommendations of the School of Social Work.[1] These recommendations included doing away with the overcrowded Aminabad center and establishing smaller, better-equipped, and better-staffed facilities to treat each kind of problem by itself. The indiscriminate mixing of children was soon replaced by separate facilities.

An orphanage for boys was subsequently established at Sina in South Teheran, and one for girls at Simetri, also in South Teheran. When Sina had been founded, as a mental hospital around 1948, patients had been kept in chains and those considered most dangerous were confined to basement cells. This facility was remodeled to serve as a child center, with fountains, grass, a new brick building, and qualified staff. In May 1973, the 250 boys in the center ranged from 11 to 16 years of age. Students from the Teheran School of Social Work have been placed at Sina since 1958. A fourth-year student is currently employed as the full-time social worker and, in May 1973, five other students were in the center for field instruction. Three advanced psychology students round out the clinical team, under the supervision of part-time psychologists and psychiatrists.

The Sina center owes a great deal to the Teheran School of Social Work, not only for program improvements and classification activities, but also for decreasing the number of children by returning some children to their homes and refusing others who should not be admitted.[2]

The institution at Simetri has one social work student. An adoption agency functioning as part of the Municipality of Teheran employs six social workers and has another six social-work students.

2. Services to delinquent children.

The separation of juveniles from adult offenders and the enactment of a juvenile court law resulted from a collaboration between Mr. Bagher Ameli and the Teheran School of Social Work.[3] Mr Ameli had been a judge and was an undersecretary of the Ministry of Justice when the School of Social Work was established. During his tenure as president of the Iranian Association for Protection of Prisoners, he had been impressed with social workers and the new School and particularly with social studies made by students at the School. In drafting the new juvenile law, based largely on the experiences of the United States and four European countries, Mr. Ameli consulted officials of the School of Social Work and incorporated their suggestions.

The new law included a permissive provision for the court to use a social worker to prepare a social study of the child and his family and to conduct research into causation. It also provided for a center to educate and train delinquents apart from adult offenders, with social workers who would make studies and suggest treatment plans at the center. Classification by sex, age, and behavior was to be carried out by social workers and temporary care for children pending disposition was to be provided.

In order to prevent untrained people from performing these tasks, one article of the new law defined a social worker as one who had a diploma from the School of Social Work.

The center has been in orperation since 1968 and is situated on the west side of Teheran. In 1973, three full-time social workers and two part-time social workers, as well as five third-year students of the School of Social Work, were active at the center. The boys served by the center average about 300, many of whom need substitute families and follow-up care by the social workers. The social workers have recommended programs to meet these needs.

Efforts are being made to add social workers to the court staffs in Teheran and to increase the social work staff in the present center. Additional centers are planned for the provincial capitals and each of them will have social workers on the staff.

3. Services to retarded children.

Social workers were instrumental in establishing two major programs to help retarded children. Less retarded children are now taught in special classes in the school system of Teheran and other cities, with a social worker playing a key role in setting up these classes and counseling parents and teachers. Since 1958, almost a hundred social work students have worked in these classes. At present, there are three part-time paid social workers and twelve literacy corpsmen.

The more retarded children are treated in a special dormitory in Razi Hospital in Teheran and other hospitals in the provinces. Successful efforts have been made to treat the more retarded children separately in order to avoid exploitation and abuse by other children and adults.

4. Social services in the schools.

Beginning in 1960, school social work services began to develop in Teheran. One of the students that year went to one of the schools in South Teheran and, in 1961, he developed an experimental program to show the value of social work in schools. The Ministry of Education was pleased with the demonstration and employed him as a permanent staff member. The number of students working in the schools grew from three in 1963 to ten in 1967. Since then, the number has fluctuated, going as low as four in 1972–1973. By 1968 the Ministry of Education had employed ten full-time social workers, although the number later decreased. Their duties included establishment of good relationships with faculty members and administrators, preparation of social studies of unadjusted students, development of treatment plans to facilitate adjustment of students, guidance of mentally retarded or deviant students, maintenance of good working relationships with parents, and referrals to social agencies.

FAMILY WELFARE
1. Family aid.

In the absence of adequate public aid, in order to meet family emergencies not provided by other services, the students felt that a Family Welfare Program was needed to handle crises.

As a pilot project, the Teheran School of Social Work established this program in 1959 in collaboration with other groups to demonstrate its need and value. It is designed to help poor families in terms of health, financial status, and social adjustment.[4] Four-fifths of the people helped are from rural areas. More than half are financially deprived.

Emergency services provided include financial grants for temporary day-to-day expenses, assistance in obtaining employment, arranging for medical and hospital care, assistance in tuition and clothing for students, and transportation expenses back to home areas.

More than 34,000 people were helped during the ten-year period of the program's existence (1959–1969), with a total expenditure of 2,814,211 rials (about $38,000). All the funds were raised by the students from faculty and friends of the School and all the services were provided by students.

Now, as the result of the demonstration, other social agencies have established larger, better funded family aid programs.

2. *Marital counseling.*

Traditionally, a Persian man could obtain a divorce in a very simple process without going to court. Mr. Ameli, after being appointed Minister of Justice in 1964, drafted a law providing for divorce only by court action after attempts at reconciliation.[5] Article 3 of this law gave the court power to obtain a study by social workers of the family background, which would help determine the course and nature of the marital problem. In addition, the law allowed women to file for divorce, provided for more equitable child support arrangements and made polygamy illegal without the consent of the first wife and the court. The Family Protection Law, enacted in 1967, received strong support from social workers and the Teheran School of Social Work.

REHABILITATION
1. *Services to beggars.*

Since 1959 the government has been dealing with the problem of beggars in the hope of reducing their numbers. Beggars, according to law, had been severely punished. The Teheran School of Social Work worked to change the attitude from one of punishment to one of rehabilitation and prevention. Training centers were established in the provincial cities to handle beggars.

Social workers have been used in the program to carry out social studies, to classify beggars by problems and needs, to establish workshops for training, to help people return to normal living, to prevent poor families from becoming beggars, and to design and plan treatment and rehabilitation programs for beggars. Subsequently, social workers have been well accepted in the numerous centers and each center has one social worker.

2. Services to prostitutes.

Prostitutes had also been sent to Aminabad when apprehended by the police. The Teheran School of Social Work took the lead in establishing a center in the red-light district of Teheran, Ghaleh Prostitution Welfare Center, to provide prostitutes with instruction in hygiene, family planning, sanitation, child care, and vocational training, as well as to offer casework services. The center's efforts are directed both at relocating prostitutes in other jobs or in marriage and at improving the living conditions of those who are unable or unwilling to leave. Since the center's establishment in 1968, 24 social work students have worked there.

Social work students have worked to establish savings accounts for the prostitutes, to ban high-interest loans, to improve health services in the "ghaleh," to control venereal disease through individual and group counseling, to arrange adult education and vocational training classes, and to treat addiction. One of the social workers estimates that most residents of the "ghaleh" are narcotics addicts and a high percentage of earnings is spent on drugs. The social workers try both to urge treatment for those who are already addicted and to prevent drug use in those who are not addicted. Especially unfortunate is the high rate of addiction among children in the "ghaleh" who have been used by pushers in the sale of drugs.

Prostitutes seldom obtain birth certificates for their children and social workers have sought to obtain them. A high percentage of the daughters of prostitutes are introduced into prostitution in their teens, and prevention programs are directed toward these young girls through the use of films, counseling, and group programs.

Another serious problem has been the introduction of married women and girls into the "ghaleh" by brokers. Formerly, this practice would lead to fights and even killings by husbands when they learned the truth, usually after contracting a venereal disease. Efforts have been made to control this problem by preventing any person from living in the "ghaleh" who does not have a card issued by the police.

The program to help prostitutes was backed by an intensive two-year survey conducted by the Teheran School of Social Work and financed by the Ministry of Interior.

3. Services to addicts.

The only hospital for addicts in Iran is located near the Teheran School of Social Work. At most times, about 120 addicts from all over the country are in residence. Social workers from the Teheran School of Social Work have been employed in the hospital over ten years, doing both group and individual counseling and about 50 students have been trained there.

Policy changes proposed by the social work staff include lengthening the treatment period from 10 to 21 days, developing a second rehabilitation center south of Teheran, establishment of a half-way house, and creation of a nationwide educational program to prevent addiction. The first proposal has been adopted and the second project has been scheduled for early construction.

Social workers and social work students have also raised funds to help addicts and their families, arranged for books and recreational facilities, planned films, assisted in planning for the return home of addicts after treatment, and worked with communities to change the public attitudes towards addicts and addiction.

4. Services to the mentally ill.

New mental health facilities, known as Razi Hospital, are located on the premises of the old Aminabad center. In 1970, a mental hospital was constructed near the University of Teheran

Medical School to be used also as a teaching center. This facility, Ruzbeh Hospital, has field work students from the Teheran School of Social Work as well as regular full-time social workers. Razi had field work students and social workers for some years and will probably have them again in the future.

5. Rehabilitation of the physically handicapped.

In 1968 the National Iranian Society for the Rehabilitation of the Disabled was created by an act of the Parliament.[6] The Society now has an intake service with a staff of twelve trained social workers to study handicapped people from the entire country and refer them to several facilities operated by the Society. These facilities include a 200-bed hospital for medical rehabilitation, which employs four social workers; a vocational assessment center, which has one social worker; a sheltered workshop with one social worker; and a vocational placement service. A total of 17,000 clients have been handled by this complex since 1968, most of whom are illiterate or partially illiterate people from financially deprived backgrounds. Many have been beggars.

The handicaps include, in order of frequency, neuromuscular difficulties such as poliomyelitis, loss of one or more limbs, and tubercular clients with bone problems or deformities.

Priority in acceptance for service is given to persons under age 26, and the highest priority is given to children under 16 on the premise that earlier treatment is more effective and more economical. Very little service is given to people over the age of 48.

The Society operates in close affiliation with the Ministry of Labor and Social Welfare, and the Ministry aids in providing a very modern program of vocational training. All graduates of the training program are placed in jobs and job turnover is very small.

Social workers not only serve in a key role as client advocates and referral agents in seeing that the handicapped clients receive their full rights to assistance and service, but also have been very helpful and influential in program development and policy change.

SOCIAL SERVICES TO WORKERS
1. Labor welfare.

The Labor Social Security Organization was one of the first organizations to accept social work activities in 1959. Students began work in 1959–1960 at Sorkhe-Hessar Tuberculosis Hospital which is under the control of the Labor Social Security Organization. In 1961 five social workers were employed at this hospital, as well as two in the children's section. A separate social work section was added to the Labor Social Security Organization in 1965, and by 1969 20 full-time social workers were employed there.

These social workers help patients adjust to the hospital and accept their illnesses. Subsequent help is provided with the social, economic and related problems of patients and their families. The social workers also interpret the regulations of the Labor Social Security Act to patients, and propose to the administration revisions and modifications of such regulations.

2. Social work in factories.

The Teheran School of Social Work began placing students in factories for their field instruction from the time the School opened. Previously, no social work had been provided in Iranian factories. Students were also placed in the labor clinics of the National Iranian Oil Company. A total of five factories have received students over the years, including an automobile assembly plant, two appliance plants, a vegetable shortening plant and a steel plant. Approximately 25 graduates of the School are now working full-time in industry.

The placement of students in the National Iranian Oil Company (NIOC) came about largely through the interest in social work of the present Prime Minister, Mr. Amir Abbas Hoveyda, who was a board member and a vice-president of NIOC early in the School's development. Students were placed in NIOC under his administrative direction. The students' tasks at the beginning were largely casework with families of factory workers, which included making arrangements for emergency loans. After a while, broader programs were developed. In 1960 the students developed a club for workers and initiated a film series.

Later, first-year students were introduced to social work at the Arj Metal Factory. By 1969 there were 23 students at Arj Factory. Casework efforts were directed toward providing a better relationship between workers and their environment.

The eclectic activities of the social worker in the Arj Factory include the following:[7]

a. Preparation of overall social service programs for the factory, including casework with employees and their families, development of programs to help workers economically, supervision of the granting of loans to employees, attention to workers' health and medical needs, and assistance and advice to employees and their relatives who are not protected by health insurance.

b. Preparation of a recreational program for the workers, including supervision of club programs, planning summer retreats for workers and their families, and planning group activities such as sports and film programs.

c. Cooperation in industrial and technical relations, including insurance and other benefits.

d. Supervision of the factory restaurant, including budgeting, responsibility for income and expenditures, auditing of accounts, monitoring of menus, and responsibility for certain supplies and equipment.

The head of Arj Factory cooperates fully with the social workers. He feels that the attention paid to the workers' health, recreation, and welfare has resulted in enhanced worker satisfaction and, hence, increased production.

A recent publication outlining the duties and responsibilities of social workers in factories in Iran noted the following:[8]

a. Study of the laborers' problems at the factory.

b. Study of the laborers' problems at home.

c. Enhancement of the laborers' knowledge through educational programs such as speech and training classes.

d. Increase in the level of production of the factory by improving the laborers' situation and developing in them an interest in their work.

e. Assistance in sports and artistic activities.
f. Assistance in social welfare through hygiene and accident security.

SOCIAL SERVICES IN THE AREA OF HOUSING

The community welfare centers have had a role in improvement of housing conditions in many of the low-income areas of Teheran and other cities. In addition, social workers are increasingly involved in urging the Ministry of Housing and Development to pay more attention to the social needs of low-income citizens rather than concentrating chiefly on the physical aspects of building programs.

During the 1972–1973 academic year, one of the first-year graduate students of the Teheran School of Social Work had her field instruction in the Ministry of Housing and Development, surveying needs of the residents of low-income apartments and public housing projects and making recommendations to Ministry officials. As an employee of the Ministry, she was able to hold a seminar to discuss her findings and recommendations and to obtain consideration of her major recommendations.

Recently, the Ministry of Housing and Development agreed to invest a million dollars in funds for the construction of community welfare centers, and it is believed that this venture into facilities for low-income citizens will lead to expanded activities in low-income housing since investment in low-income housing has been recognized as a priority need by the government.

Non-governmental housing organizations are also supporting construction of community welfare centers and are becoming interested in low-income housing.

VIII   Other Social Services in Rural Areas

BACKGROUND OF EFFORTS IN RURAL AREAS

A rural development program was begun by the government coinciding with the opening of the Teheran School of Social Work in 1958. Most of the people in Iran were living in rural areas—between 70 and 75 percent—and it was felt that a rural development program would reach a majority of the population.

The first year, four students were sent to villages on the outskirts of Teheran which were chosen for several reasons. The land, which had belonged to the Government, was among the first to be distributed to the farmers and, with land ownership, the farmers here had a greater independence than they did in villages still owned by landlords. Furthermore, landlords were likely to cause trouble for anyone trying to effect social change in villages they owned. In addition, the *Omrane Dehat* (a government agency for rural community development) had been active in this area and had already trained *dehyars* or village level workers. *Omrane Dehat* had laid the foundation for the School and made it possible for the students to continue training village workers. Over the years, the School of Social Work has trained some 50 to 60 development agents of the Ministry of Interior's Department of Rural Community Development. However, where *Omrane Dehat* had stressed physical development, such as the building of sanitary facilities, the social workers' emphasis was on human development, on first preparing the village residents for the physical changes in their situation.

Every year since 1958, the School has sent about ten students to work in rural areas, although the areas themselves have changed. In some cases, the distinctive character of the village necessitates the selection of a student who will be able to fit in culturally or linguistically. For example, the roughly 700 people who live in one village near Teheran speak Turkish as their first language. (Many people in this area are of Turkish origin.) A student who speaks Turkish stands a better chance of being accepted and trusted by the villagers.

Once the people in a particular area have become accustomed to the work of the social workers and have learned to deal more effectively with their own problems, the School transfers its activities to new communities. Proximity to Teheran and the availbility of transportation both to and between the villages have also been important considerations in choosing locations. In addition, areas in which the farmers own their own land are preferable. Since 1967, the School has been sending students to the villages in Karadj which is near the city of Teheran.

These students take a community development and self-help approach aimed at acquainting rural people with measures and programs for better health, sanitation, family planning, and also aimed at raising their incomes, through more and better crops, and raising their level of literacy. They first familiarize themselves, with the cultural, religious, historic, economic and geographical characteristics of the village to which they are assigned. The student social workers use their classroom training to evaluate, jointly with the villagers, the strengths, weaknesses, capacities and problems in their villages. Then, building on the strengths, they help the villagers to overcome problems. The students also try to become acquainted with the village councilmen and other community leaders such as the *mullah* or religious leader. At times, they may try to meet the landlord or his agent in instances where the village is partially or wholly owned by a landlord. (Land reform still allows the ownership of one village.)

The work of the students in the rural welfare program has been in four areas:

1. Work with the village council.
2. Work with youth.

3. Work with women and their husbands.
4. Work with other rural organizations.

1. Work with the village council.

The village councils, which came into existence after land reform, are responsible for all activities taking place at the village level. The students have worked with them particularly on physical development, such as the building of water pipes, sanitary facilities, roads, mosques, schools and clinics.

Since teamwork and community development were unknown in the villages, a good deal of the effort of student social workers went into encouraging joint responsibility and initiative. Before land reform, the landlord made the basic decisions and the people were dependent upon him for food, housing, administration of justice, and patterns of living. Since land reform and the loss of an authoritarian leader, the people had often been unable to get together to make even simple decisions.

Thus the work of the students was to show them how to work as a team, to come together and discuss, argue, negotiate, allocate responsibility and demand their rights. Various methods, including casework, group work and community work, were used to help the villagers overcome these difficulties in human relations and create a cooperative spirit. Once these problems were overcome, the village councils had to be shown how to get in touch with higher administrative officials and bodies to implement their programs. In many places the students were successful in creating team efforts and the results have included new schools, roads and baths built with village labor and without government subsidy. In areas where the individual owner rendered the village council ineffective, the students have tried to find development projects of mutual interest to landlord and tenant, such as the building of a road.

2. Work with youth.

Problems between generations exist in rural as well as urban areas, particularly in villages close to Teheran where mass communications and easy transportation to the city are available.

Student social workers, through group discussions and individual conferences, try to establish better communication between young people and their parents, as well as to develop in the village youth a sense of belonging to the community. In addition, programs for young people are organized to help them make better use of their leisure time and to encourage socialization. Among the means have been sports programs, a library group and, where possible, a television club. The social workers also discuss with youth their future career aspirations and help clarify plans for education and training.

3. Work with women and their husbands.

In 1958 the Teheran School of Social Work offered the first formal course in Iran on population problems and family planning. When the students were confronted with the problems posed by population growth, they began to focus on family planning in their field work and to diffuse these ideas in rural areas. In the first area the School worked in, the time and the people were not yet ready for these concepts. The second location where students worked was a very religious place due to the presence of a shrine, and not until the School moved to a third area could a family planning clinic be opened. The clinic served as a base for operations in the surrounding villages and students were sent out to motivate people to use contraceptives and inform them of the services offered by the clinic.

In 1967 the School moved its activities to villages west of Teheran. The time and the people were by then sufficiently advanced to enable the development of a comprehensive program to bring family planning services to rural families, many of whom had had little or no access to contraceptive devices before.

However, only male students could be sent to the villages to work with the parents and they were unable to discuss family planning with rural women directly. The School suggested to the Family Planning Association that they cooperate on a joint project to train young village girls as motivators. Eleven girls, all primary school graduates between the ages of 18 and 25, were selected and each was to be assigned to the village in which she lived. It was felt that a local girl would have the advantage of knowing the local dialect as well as the customs and attitudes of the village women. To ensure acceptance, the motivator is in each case related to a village leader whose support could thus also be counted upon. Village councils were also consulted in the selection of a motivator, additionally broadening the base of her support and the understanding of her aims.

The motivators attended a two-week training course, and when they completed the course, the local Governor presented their certificates in the presence of influential community members, whose support will later be enlisted. Once a month a refresher course is held for all motivators at the Association headquarters. At this time questions and problems which have arisen during the month can be discussed with doctors and social workers.

A supervisory committee decided that the motivators should work under the supervision of the social work students, rather than under the medical personnel who would be concerned primarily with the clinical aspects of family planning. The motivators concentrate instead on the human relations aspects of family planning, bringing the families together with the social workers, midwives, and physicians and informing them of the available clinical facilities. Most importantly, they work to educate the people, for without an understanding of the importance of family planning for the general welfare of the family, people will not be motivated to continue using contraceptives.

In each of the ten villages in the program, a one or two room center was set up in the home of the motivator. The motivators, with the help of a social work student, began their work by preparing an index for their village, listing the number of families, number of children in each family, number of women of fertile age, and recording the births, weddings and deaths. During the home visits to survey the community, they told the women what would be offered to them: educational sessions, visits from doctors and midwives, family planning information and devices.

A mobile team, donated by IPPF in 1970 and consisting of a midwife, an audio-visual man, and a driver, travels between villages in a Land Rover equipped with audio-visual facilities. The mobile unit visits each village twice a month. Meanwhile, the motivators are responsible for making appointments for the midwife to see new acceptors, acceptors due for their semiannual or annual check-ups, and acceptors complaining of side effects. Records and a monthly report for the supervisory committee are prepared by the motivator under the close supervision of the midwife. To ensure a high continuation rate, motivators are responsible for visiting all acceptors every month. If difficulties arise, they arrange for the women to be seen by the midwife in a nearby village. Motivators are kept informed of the mobile unit's schedule in case of emergency.

In addition, they invite mothers in groups of 15 to 20 to attend educational sessions run by the midwife of the mobile unit and the social work student. These sessions cover various topics including maternal and child health, environmental health, and the social and economic implications of family planning. In some villages, for the first time this year, men and women have attended lectures on family planning together. The motivators continue the teaching of simple concepts of sanitation, hygiene and child care when they visit the village women. In addition, some attempt has been made to have the motivators teach literacy in their visits.

*4. Work with other institutions
and organizations at the village level.*

Various government programs operate at the village level, but the representatives of these organizations are unfamiliar with the rural way of life, with the people and their traditions. Moreover, the people themselves are not ready to make use of the programs designed to help them. Neither one has any idea of the resources of the other. The job of the student social worker is to familiarize each with the other, to try to establish links so that the best use can be made of the available resources.

SPECIFIC ACCOMPLISHMENTS

In one village near Teheran, past trouble between the landlord and the farmers has led to continued disputes. Village land is owned both by the landlord and the villagers and the village council is largely inoperative due to the conflicts between the two. Yet even under these inauspicious conditions, the efforts of a social work student have led to striking improvements, including the initiation of a library in the mosque (where the traffic is greater than it would be in an independent location), the planning of a park to be built in the coming year, and the donation of local funds for a roadbuilding project. Furthermore, by working through the parent-teacher association, he has brought about the reopening of the local school which had been closed due to landlord-peasant strife. Much of the progress in this village has resulted from the cooperation of the *mullah* and the leadership of the village councilmen.

The villages between Teheran and Karadj illustrate the impact of student social workers as well as the continued heavy hand of the landlord. In the peasant-owned village, the children play happily on the sides of the streets or in vacant lots, the sewers (*jubes*) are clean, trees have been planted, and housewives industriously work to clean their houses, lawns, and clothing. Many houses have been freshly painted and display new house numbers. Here, the social worker has been successful in creating at atmosphere of cooperation and initiative so that the villagers can meet both personal and civic needs.

But before any cooperative effort could be achieved, the social worker, over a period of years, had to heal a breach between the two extended families that dominated the village. Recently, a school has been built, a 2,000 book library has been started, a cooperative has been established, a public bath constructed, and the use of electricity is being planned through local effort.

A nearby landlord-owned village presented a striking contrast in November 1972. The children were dull and apathetic. The *jubes* were dirty. There were no trees or shrubs and the village appeared drab and dusty. Houses were ill-kept and little evidence of cleaning or painting could be seen. The social worker was initially so discouraged that strong support from his supervisor was necessary before any kind of progress could begin. But, by March 1973, a PTA had been organized in the school, a library had been started, and the public bath had opened. The water supply has been improved and the village itself presents a cleaner appearance.

In some villages, many people were addicted to opium, a tradition dating back to an earlier period in Iran's history. The socila work students tried to cure and rehabilitate the addicts by sending them to hospitals. Older people, still attached to traditional patterns, were given opium allotments from government sources in order to stop the activity of peddlars in gaining new addicts among younger people while supplying older people.

METHODOLOGY AND PROCESS

The literature on community development has stressed self-help, with the thrust being at the local level with local autonomy paramount.[1] But more recent analyses have stressed that community development cannot substitute for basic social provisions and that community development can optimally be closely related to national policies and resources.[2]

The students of the Teheran School of Social Work, as well as graduates in later employment, have been most effective when their methodology has moved all the way from the initial study to implementation with a close relationship *both* with villagers and with representatives of ministries concerned with health, education, welfare, and related programs.

Perhaps the community development worker is essentially most helpful in a brokerage role in which he establishes a link between people and resource systems.[3] This may explain the successes attained in Iran in the areas of construction of educational and recreational facilities and planning of new programs. In many instances, consultation and funds were secured from national ministries, and in any case these are the kind of improvements strongly endorsed by national policy.

A typical process might involve the following steps: (1) general orientation into the specific village by a supervisor and introduction to key government officials and village leaders; (2) a series of contacts on a person-to-person basis with government officials and village leaders until a working relationship is established; (3) meanwhile, other villagers are contacted and become well-known to the student; (4) priority needs are assessed in individual meetings with village leaders, government officials, and villagers and subsequently ratified in group meetings; (5) detailed plans are developéd, including plans to obtain funds from either governmental sources or from local sources or, most often, a combination of the two; (6) the plans are discussed and ratified in both individual and group meetings with village leaders, villagers, and government officials; (7) procedures are established for coordination, monitoring and evaluation of the work, as well as actual performance of the work.

Conclusions and Recommendations

Unfortunately, field placements of the Teheran School of Social Work are difficult to maintain further than 30 or 40 kilometers from Teheran, so that only part of Iran's villages have been able to benefit from pilot projects including summer block placements.

Another difficulty is in arranging placements for women social work students in rural villages, even those close to Teheran. So far only men have been utilized, with one or two exceptions, but studies and experiments are being made to determine how best to introduce women social workers as community development personnel in the villages.

The most serious problem, however, is that social workers prefer to work in Teheran or other cities after graduation, even when their field placements have been in villages. Continuity of service is, therefore, difficult to achieve, and the hope of developing a national social work service in villages is still unrealized. It may be necessary to provide very strong incentives to overcome the attractions of city life, such as substantial increases in salary, free furnished quarters, free access to automobiles, and frequent vacations.

In all classes at the Teheran School of Social Work it is emphasized that the major thrust of the social worker's efforts must be in rural areas. Students doing field work in rural areas must spend nights in the villages and remain in the villages for three months during the summer. Before the celebrations for the 2,500th Anniversary in 1971, students worked in villages around Persepolis from March to October, helping with village development: reform, reconstruction, re-education. They received a prize from the Shah for their efforts.

From the beginning the School has tried to emphasize the importance of work in rural areas. About half the students do return to the provinces, although many of this number remain in provincial cities and towns rather than going to rural areas. One answer to the problem of rural services has been the training at the Teheran School of Social Work of approximately 50 *dehyars* who have been on scholarship from the Ministries of Health and of Rural Development. These *dehyars*, or rural community development workers, are now in charge of training programs to prepare other *dehyars* for rural areas.

Perhaps one effective way of insuring services to the rural areas of Iran will be to work through the education, health, and development corps who are already deployed in some of the rural villages. It is hoped that later all villages will be covered by the corpsmen. If social work philosophy and approaches can be taught to the revolutionary corps, the country's rural areas can receive adequate social services much more quickly than directly from social workers alone.

The Teheran School of Social Work is, nonetheless, demonstrating the value of community development work in the villages, and the government has indicated a strong interest in extending community development to all the nations' villages. The School has succeeded in convincing the government that village development personnel need some amount of social work training. The Fourth Development Plan envisioned the establishment of village councils in all villages and increased expenditures on public utilities and sanitation.[4] Hence, the government has been able simply to channel funds through the councils that have been established, and has relied largely on village initiative in carrying out these policies. Thus, to implement these self-help programs, it is of the utmost importance to train and deploy a large cadre of qualified community development personnel who view village development as a permanent career. In the Fifth Plan, the government indicated that a half million villagers engaged in village organizations or councils would receive short-term training.[5]

During the 1973–1974 academic year, more students were added to the rural program. So far, each student has been assigned to only one village. But it is felt that students are capable of handling more than one village. Thus, the program can be expanded to reach more villages. In addition, the family planning aspects of the program have won the support of UNFPA and this support will enable the training of motivators and the establishment of a mobile unit to reach more villages.

IMPLICATIONS OF THE IRAN EXPERIENCE FOR OTHER COUNTRIES

Social work students will encounter better reception in rural areas if their initial thrust is the improvement of such physical resources as water pipes, sanitary facilities, and roads. Later, the emphasis can be shifted gradually to human development and, specifically, to family planning.

A more lasting impact will result if the village leadership is involved throughout both the planning and action processes, since the basic objective is to build a permanent problem-solving capability rather than to solve specific problems alone.

The work of the motivator, a local primary school graduate, has been particularly crucial to the success of family planning in the rural areas in Iran. The motivator approaches women at their own level of understanding and cultural values. She is important in follow-up, evaluation and reinforcement, in addition to motivation for family planning, and she also plays a role in the teaching of hygiene, sanitation, and child care.

Women comprise a particularly receptive group for family planning efforts in rural areas, since most of the women welcome help in planning smaller families as well as help with hygiene, sanitation, diet and child care. When initial efforts are directed at women, it is sometimes possible to include men in the groups at a later date.

The suggestions we have for countries in which land reform has not been carried out, or only partially effected, is that villages which are largely or entirely in small ownership be singled out as priority areas to demonstrate social change and social reform. A second suggestion, if few or no villages are in small ownership, is to work directly with the landlord or his agent to enlist his cooperation or at least to dilute his opposition.

The single village is often not large enough and does not have the necessary resources to serve as a basis for overall rural development. Construction of such social service facilities as schools and dispensaries on a village basis may be of dubious value because of the generally poor quality of service and the high cost of operation. Attention is being given to regional and zonal approaches to development, which can overcome the disadvantages of village development alone, tapping the superior resources of the national government while retaining the participation of local authorities in decision-making.[6]

Since most villages in Iran contain between 50 and 350 families, it is impractical either to send a social worker to each village or to build facilities in each village. What the government has been working on is a satellite program in which one slightly larger village is provided with resources such as a school, recreational facilities, and health services. A social worker would be based here and would travel during the day to outlying villages. The government has agreed to this plan, and some experimental work has been accomplished. The revolutionary corps, who have four months of training before being sent out to rural areas, do receive lectures on social work methods: how to work with people and how to accept them. But they do not receive in-depth preparation in social work.

PART B
The Teheran School of Social Work

The following chapter is addressed specifically to the historical evolution of the Teheran School of Social Work and to a description of how the school has attempted to respond to the changes that are occurring in the country as a result of the White Revolution. It should be noted that the school began in 1958, several years before the initiation of the White Revolution. But the school's objectives, curriculum, and priorities were affected by the overall social needs pinpointed by the White Revolution, many of which had been articulated by the Shah and governmental officials well before 1962.

IX   Preparation of Social Workers to Man the Social Welfare Programs of the Revolution

THE DEVELOPMENT OF SOCIAL SERVICES IN IRAN

Traditionally charity was largely handled through giving a fifth to a tenth of one's income to the poor as a religious obligation, although a person's principal obligation is to his family.[1] The first organized social service in the country was the Red Lion and Sun Society, the Iranian counterpart of the Red Cross, established in 1923.[2] It has 135 branches throughout the country, providing flood, fire and earthquake relief, as well as being engaged in some 350 charity operations such as counseling centers for mothers and infants, blood banks, orphanages, clinics, and hospitals.[3] More than two decades later, a series of other services was initiated, including the Imperial Organization for Social Services and the Foundation for the Protection of Mother and Child.[4] The main efforts of the former are directed at improving health conditions and offering free health care to low-income families.[5] The latter maintains maternity clinics and facilities for premature infants.

With rising concern about poverty, ill health, child neglect, crime, addiction and other social problems which proliferated with urbanization and industrialization, additional voluntary agencies were formed in the 1940's and 1950's. These included the Pahlavi Foundation, the Society for the Protection of Prisoners, the Society for the Protection of Children, the Farah Pahlavi

119

Charitable Foundation, and the Higher Council of Social Welfare. The Pahlavi Foundation, based on the Crown Endowment of the Shah, was established in 1961 to support a program of low-rent housing construction, moderately priced restaurants for workers, assistance to student hostels, scholarships, cultural projects, and other activities of interest to the Shah.[6] The Society for the Protection of Prisoners extends aid to the families of needy prisoners and maintains workshops, recreation halls, tuberculosis centers and narcotics control centers for prisoners. The Society for the Protection of Children operates an adoptive service as well as residential facilities for dependent children and for retarded child ren. It also provides milk and lunches for school children from low-income families.[7] The Farah Pahlavi Charitable Foundation provides care for indigent, abandoned and orphaned children. The Higher Council of Social Welfare has now been incorporated into the Ministry of Social Welfare.

In 1948 Plan Organization was created, using a share of the nation's oil resources to direct the economic and social development of the nation.[8] Plan Organization stimulated the passage of a number of social welfare laws, under the administration of various government ministries.

By the middle fifties, public and private organizations had developed a number of social welfare programs for various groups including orphans, beggars and vagrants, criminals and delinquents, as well as programs in rural community development, labor welfare, and welfare services in hospitals and clinics. All of these services were staffed by academically untrained social welfare personnel. No research-based assessments of effectiveness are available, but a lack of professional career development resulted in problems of high staff turnover, lack of accountability and relatively low salary and prestige. Most of these agencies were in Teheran and other larger cities, and most of the nation's population was not reached.

Government ministries, private charitable organizations, philanthropic individuals and concerned citizens began to see some advantages in preparation of better educated social workers to man the social agencies in the country. Among these groups were

Plan Organization, the Ministry of Labor, the Imperial Organization for Social Services, and the Pahlavi Foundation.

ESTABLISHMENT OF THE TEHERAN SCHOOL OF SOCIAL WORK

At this time, various governmental bodies and voluntary organizations sought help from the International Labor Office and other branches of the United Nations to evaluate and recommend directions for social policy and services, particularly for the Social Insurance Program, as well as to suggest patterns for training social work personnel in the handling of Social Insurance. But the most influential evaluation was made by a 1955 United Nations team headed by Mr. Arthur Altmayer, one of the architects of the Social Security Act in the United States, and including Miss Sattarah Farman-Farmaian, who was an Iranian UN Social Welfare advisor to the Government of Iraq.

That team recommended the establishment of a school of social work to train qualified personnel to man the burgeoning social services in the country.

A specific program and plan to implement these early studies was presented in March, 1958 by Miss Farman-Farmaian, who held a Master's degree in Social Work from the University of Southern California as well as a degree in education, and was at that time the only Iranian professionally trained in social work. The plan included a two-year program of study at the undergraduate level leading to a diploma for qualified graduates of secondary schools. The plan also called for the new school to be government-sponsored and operated under a constitution approved by the Higher Council of Education, but it would also have independent status as a private, voluntary institution.[9]

The Iranian government accepted the plan and appointed Miss Farman-Farmaian director of the new school. The board of directors was formed in the summer of 1958, with the Minister of the Imperial Court serving as chairman as well as liaison between the School and the government. On July 15, 1958 the School was given official status as an approved educational institution by the Higher Council of Education of the Ministry of Education.

In the beginning, the profession of social work was so new

that many terms had to be coined. Even the word for social work had to be introduced into the Persian language. Recruitment of students was initially through advertisements in newspapers. No one really knew what the school would offer when he arrived. Some students were attracted by the words "social service" in the School's name. More recently, guidance counselors in the high schools are introducing students to the profession of social work.

The first academic year began in October 1958 with twenty students. Courses were offered in casework, group work, community organization, personality and mental hygiene, family structure, rural welfare, statistics and research, medical information, sanitation, nutrition, 'and English. Field instruction in community agencies was initiated. Part-time Iranian faculty took responsibility for teaching the basic courses, while foreign professional social workers from community agencies taught methods courses and helped in field instruction at first. It was primarily the casework orientation of these foreigners that caused the casework emphasis of the school in the early days. In 1960 the Teheran School of Social Work was accepted for membership in the International Association of Schools of Social Work in recognition of the quality of its curriculum.

From the outset, requests were made to the United Nations and the Fulbright Commission for consultants and advisors who could help in curriculum planning and particularly in the teaching of social work methods. The United Nations has furnished a total of eight consultants and instructors during a period extending over ten years. The Fulbright Commission has sent seven consultants and lecturers, and continues to support the School. The help of the consultants and advisors has been particularly valuable in view of the paucity of professionally educated social workers in Iran in the early years, and specifically in view of the lack of qualified social work educators in the country. Outstanding contributions were made in curriculum development, teacher training, and administrative counsel. The School has always made use of foreigners in Teheran who have professional education and experience in social work. Among international agencies who have furnished part-time personnel from time to time are the American Joint Distribution Committee and the United Presbyterian Church in the U.S.A. (Commission on Ecumenical Mission and Relations). The Peace Corps has furnished several lecturers, chiefly as teachers of English. The Norwegian Volunteer Group and various other international volunteer groups have also aided the School.

During the first four years of the School's existence, one program of study was offered: the two-year curriculum leading to a diploma awarded by the Ministry of Education. During this period, extensive efforts were made to familiarize government agencies with the role of social workers and social work education through literature, speeches and the work of the students. Acquainting the country with the new profession became the first order of business.

By the 1962–1963 academic year, the diploma program had achieved sufficient integrity and stability to allow the School to initiate a second, higher level of training. In the additional program, selected candidates who had graduated from the diploma program were given a third year of education which led to a licentiate awarded by the Ministry of Education. Since Iran offered a licentiate, equivalent to a bachelor's degree, after three years at the university level, the School adopted the pattern already approved for the nation.

In 1963, the School again reviewed its academic program with the advice and counsel of Dr. Eileen Blackey, then Dean of the UCLA School of Social Work, and Dr. Katherine A. Kendall, now Secretary General of the International Association of Schools of Social Work, and, with the approval of the Higher Council of the Ministry of Education, extended the baccalaureate programs to four years. This was in accordance with the program of all national universities.

As social work became better known and the student body grew ten-fold,[10] the need for teachers, field instructors and administrators became acute. Thus, in 1970, as a result of faculty studies and the assistance of graduates and foreign consultants to evaluate directions of the School, the Higher Council approved the School's proposal to offer a two-year M.S.W. curriculum in social work teaching, research and administration.

As is usual with graduates of schools of social work, the career choices after graduation are wide and varied, as indicated in Chart II.

EARLY DAYS OF THE SCHOOL

As recalled by one of the first students, the school started in 1958 with one room in a dark basement provided by the Ministry of Labor. Later the school moved to two rooms upstairs in the same building, and in another six months to a rented house which lacked adequate classroom space. When the third year was added to the curriculum in 1962, the army was asked to build temporary classroom quarters. They were, however, primitive and without insulation. In 1963, the present well-designed and adequate building was constructed, and the Family Planning Association annex was opened in 1968. The Community Welfare Center was also housed on campus after its incorporation in 1970.

The lack of teaching materials, including textbooks, has been a major problem throughout the history of the school. In the beginning there were no local materials and no translations. Translation of social work materials were extremely difficult because translators were unfamiliar with social work terminology, much of which had just been coined. The western textbooks and a few case records, which were used initially, created numerous problems, not only in terms of the different cultural interpretations of behavior but also because the organizations available to provide services were so different. Persian students often failed to understand the cases. The methods teachers and field instructors were all foreigners, except for the School's director who was also teaching and supervising. Language problems, cultural barriers, and all kinds of difficulties in communication abounded. Superior students were called upon at times to mediate between teachers and translators.

The foreign faculty was not familiar with the culture. Two examples of the ensuing problems have been provided by one of the first students. A group work teacher began with programming and showed the students how to play. She had the entire class holding hands and jumping up and down, horrifying the rather formal and reserved Persian students. They had difficulty taking either the teacher or the content seriously.

When one of the early students was doing his field work at an installation of the National Iranian Oil Company, he counseled an attractive 18-year old girl who invited him to make a home visit. He declined since he did not know the husband and did not have his approval. When the incident came up for discussion in supervisory conference, the western supervisor began helping the student with what she considered to be his problem, i. e., the fact that he had been reared in a society which segregated the sexes and therefore he was uncomfortable in working with the opposite sex. The student tried to explain that if he had gone to the girl's home, the neighbors, who had never even heard of a social worker, would have spread rumors and a scandal might well have developed. However, the student was never able to convince the supervisor that he really enjoyed working with the opposite sex under culturally acceptable circumstances.

The research staff was made up not of social researchers but of mathematicians and statisticians who filled their courses with mathematics and statistics and largely ignored social problems. The research staff had no idea of course objectives or the relationship of the course to the curriculum. Research studies contained a hundred pages of tables to perhaps ten pages of analysis and evaluation. Gradually, the research teaching improved to the point that the community welfare centers, services for prostitutes and services for children in the courts were all developed largely on the basis of research done by students at the school.

Part-time instructors at first refused to prepare course outlines, considering such a request as an infringement on academic freedom. So at first the curriculum was extremely hard to balance or even to understand or predict.

Community acceptance was a serious problem in the early days. People were suspicious and resisted in various ways. When students went to one agency near a vegetable market, they were pelted with tomatoes and potatoes. In another section, they were stoned. Some people refused to talk to students at all, believing they were connected with the police. The first generation of students became known as "The Bulldozers," in that they paved the way for later students.

Students were sometimes physically thrown out of homes and offices. The school director had to retrieve students from jail on a number of occasions. In one factory briefing, a student was thought to be flirting with the women and was beaten up. At various times students were thought to be spying, to be policing the factory's activities, to be interfering with workers. When they were able to find field placements, students were not given any office space to work in, and often had to bring their own chairs and sit in the garden. The Board Chairman, who had been Minister of Court during the school's first years, held weekly meetings with government officials to explain the functions of the school. The students themselves were the best agents in overcoming the resistance that was encountered. Parents were grateful for what had been done for their children by the students. Families of students interpreted the purposes of the school. Students brought their own friends and relatives to aid in the growth of the student body. Students accepted responsibility for briefing officials and residents in communities where they had their field instruction.

Since no one had ever heard of a social worker when the School opened, field work placements were hard to find and develop. But later, once the profession was established, other agencies began offering short courses for a few months in an effort to move toward identification with the social work profession. The railroad taught employees, calling them social workers, to offer cold drinks to people who fainted on trains. The Mayor of Teheran developed a six-week training course in social work for cleaning women and nursery attendants in municipal orphanages. No professional organization of social workers existed to develop job levels related to tasks, but the government agency handling personnel policies was provided with job descriptions and qualifications. As soon as the first class was graduated from the School, a professional organization was founded.

DEVELOPMENT OF CURRICULUM

Schools of social work in all developing countries have tended to base their curriculum on the western model, with some concessions to local conditions.[11] This tendency has probably been closely related to the scarcity of indigenous teaching materials, a lack of systematically developed literature in comparative curriculum-building based on different social structures and societal needs, and rather superficial thinking about the universality of human nature and individual human needs.

Although the initial curriculum followed the western model fairly closely, a number of emerging needs gradually led to reassessment and redesigning of the curriculum. It became clear, for example, that widespread employment opportunities did not exist in Iran for social workers prepared exclusively or even primarily to give diagnostic and therapeutic interviews in office settings. The issue of how to deliver professional services in a developing country has gradually deviated from the classical model of therapeutic services to individual middle-class clients. The early, and particularly later, social services in Iran militated toward a more comprehensive role for the social workers, in which intervention included educational, research, coordinating, and other components.

The curriculum needed to be geared to meeting pressing needs which had less to do with emotional needs than with physical health and the physical environment, i.e., creating a better and more sanitary environment was the primary objective. Students had to deal with the basic needs of the people: sewage and garbage disposal, sanitation, cleanliness, family planning. In some cases they had to show how to perform such simple tasks as opening a window and to explain why this might be advisable. A curriculum suitable for developed countries was obviously inappropriate. Students who intended to help community residents to clean a street did not have a priority need to know the principles of psychiatric social work. Rather, the immediate need was to be taught nutritional values and the basics of public health. Thus, the curriculum was geared to the basic problems of health, education, and welfare in Iran.

Since these were the first socal work students in the history
of Iran and the whole concept was completely new to the country, the curriculum could not go immediately to casework, group
work and community organization. These methods were too
sophisticated. The School wanted instead to prepare general social
workers who could help people with health, education, and environmental problems. The curriculum was thus geared to general
problem-solving, whether with an employer, a family member,
the government, or whomever. This approach continues even today. When the two-year program was increased to four years,
social work methods courses were introduced. Yet the School
continues to develop generic social workers with field instruction
in villages, schools, community welfare centers, and orphanages
—facilitating practice in a specific context.

Since there was only one trained social worker in the country
when the School opened, there were no social work materials.
Funds were allocated for preparation of materials in the related
areas of nursing, public health, nutrition, medicine, and the social
sciences. During the first year, a book of indigenous cases was
prepared by a North American social worker, in Iran as a UN
technical assistance representative and published in English and
Persian. The faculty, with the help of UN and Fulbright personnel, developed teaching case material. Background studies and
instruction manuals for field instructors have been published.
Several faculty members have written textbooks and research
monographs.

In a country in which there is but one new school of social
work and one professionally educated social worker—as the situation was in Iran in 1958—the new school has a unique opportunity to shape practice as well as to shape the direction of social
work education. And, since very soon after the establishment of
the new school, the White Revolution was initiated, the School
also had an opportunity to use itself planfully to help deal with
changes resulting from the new national policy.

The structuring of new agencies, new programs, and new jobs
therefore became a major component of the development of the
Teheran School of Social Work. Since jobs of social workers tend
to determine perceptions and preferences regarding people, prob-

lems, outcomes and methods, the School could not only prepare students educationally but also help them to continue in a new and emerging kind of practice related directly to implementation of the social objectives of the White Revolution.[12]

Actually, as Harbison and Myers have pointed out: "The social and political pressures for education are powered by economic motivations. And for this reason an educational system which fails to prepare persons for available jobs is . . . by any definition inefficient."[13] The Teheran School of Social Work was obligated to develop a new panoply of jobs for its graduates, and the creation of the system of family planning clinics (Chapter V), community welfare centers (Chapter VI), other urban social work jobs (Chapter VII) and village community developers (Chapter VIII) can be understood both as the effort to deal with social changes resulting from the White Revolution and as the development of jobs for the graduates of the School.

The establishment of the Teheran School of Social Work independently of the university can be best understood in the light of its conception as an instrument to help deal with extensive social changes in Iran and in the light of the need to use the School to help develop a viable system of social services for the country. Herman Stein has pointed out the implicit strain between the university's role as center of learning, with a paramount commitment to freedom in teaching and research, and, on the other hand, a profession's role of responsiveness to societal needs.[14] Although he concluded that the professional school can be highly compatible with the academic tradition of the university, the particular context of societal needs and the greater freedom of an independent professional school to meet those needs induced the leadership of the Teheran School of Social Work to take an independent direction at least in its early years. Similarly, the necessity to place priority on the development of new social services, coupled with the strong preference for work in Teheran and vicinity on the part of the School's graduates has slowed down the time-consuming process of planning other schools of social work in provincial cities of the country.

Even more cogently, the economic, social, and political realities of poverty, extensive migration to the cities, poor housing, inadequate diet, ill health, and illiteracy forced the School to consider broader approaches to the preparation of social workers. These broader approaches related more to thrusts aimed at changing social policies, social institutions, public attitudes, and other aspects of the social structure, than to programs aimed at changing individual perceptions and relationships alone. Even at the individual and family level, the stress needed to be on helping mothers realize the importance of a balanced diet and of the elementary rules of hygiene as well as the more traditional emphasis on encouragement of a more understanding parent-child relationship.

Over the school's existence, then, social workers tended to be prepared for roles such as administrator, teacher, trainer, supervisor, coordinator, organizer, planner rather than as caseworker in the traditional sense. Even graduates going into casework positions found themselves providing a variety of educational, guidance, leadership, advocate, ombudsman, and facilitating functions rather than serving as diagnostician-therapist.

As suggested earlier, in a real sense the social work curriculum in a developing country becomes itself in part an instrument for attacking some of the key social problems of the country. What were the paramount social problems of Iran in the late 1950s when the School was established and in the 1960s when the School was developing? The following, all related to the objectives of the White Revolution, were among the most critical and pressing:

1. Population growth.

Although Iran had perhaps a total population of six million in the 1870s, by 1966 the picture had changed drastically under the impact of urbanization, industrialization, and improved standards of health and nutrition. By 1966, the population was almost 26 million, and unless the approximately 3.2 percent annual growth is curtailed, estimates are that Iran's population will reach 100,-000,000 in the early 2000s.[15]

2. Rural-to-urban migration.

Discussed at more length in Chapter VI, the spread of urbanization in Iran and rising expectations in the villages has led to an accelerating migration of people to the cities. Poorly prepared educationally, vocationally, culturally and even physically, these migrants have settled in extremely poor sections of major cities, particularly Teheran, where facilities and services are lacking.

3. *Illiteracy.*

In the 1956 census only 22.2 percent of all males (45.2 percent of urban males and 10.8 percent of rural males) and only 7.3 percent of all females (20.6 percent of urban females and 1.0 percent of rural females) were literate in the population ten years and over. By the 1966 census, under the impact of the White Revolution, the literacy rate had reached 40.6 percent of all males (62.3 percent urban and 25.6 rural) and 18.0 percent of females (38.4 percent and 4.3 percent rural).[16]

4. *Inequality of women in social, economic and political spheres.*

The traditional place of womne in Persian society has been largely one of childbearing and child-rearing. Women were given the opportunity to vote only very recently. Education has been largely for men and boys. Women have been allowed to enter into employment in large numbers for a very few decades. Among the many results of this condition of inequality have been the poor levels of child care and child training in the home, an inadequate understanding of hygiene and nutrition, and the communication of a circumscribed world view and set of values to children.

5. *The peasants' lack of experience in decision-making.*

The rural population of Iran, still the bulk of the total population, has lived chiefly in villages dominated by landlords and their agents. All decisions were made by the landlords or his agent, and peasants entered the White Revolution with no background in decision-making, social mobility, political participation, or even education.

6. *Inadequate work skills for an industrializing economy.*

The poorer classes in Iran have not generally had access to vocational schools and other opportunities to acquire work skills that would prepare them for positions in industry.

7. *Poor diet and nutrition.*

The poorer classes have not had access to educational opportunities that would enable them to learn the rudiments of nutrition, balanced diet, and care of food. Nor has there been enough food for many, even most, families in view of the traditional inequality in distribution of resources. The United Nations has pointed out the overriding priority that should be attached to nutrition, particularly of children.[17]

8. *Poor housing, hygiene and sanitation.*

In the villages, and in poorer sections of the cities, the housing has been grossly inadequate. Problems of inadequate sewage disposal, unavailability of clean water, and lack of cleanliness, have been added to housing conditions characterized by insufficient space and facilities, to produce a high rate of disease and chronic disability.

The Teheran School of Social Work addressed itself increasingly to the tasks of establishing new social services, stimulating the enactment of new laws and the formulation of new policies, and developing an appropriate curriculum to prepare social work personnel, that would together attack problems whose alleviation was perceived as vital to the achievement of the goals of the White Revolution. The Shah has stressed the reduction of social and economic inequalities as the path toward social justice, and these various social problems all stemmed from basic inequalities. For example, population growth would not be a serious problem if women were not expected to have large families as their sole avenue to social status and prestige.

The activities of the School, its faculty and its student body were increasingly directed toward the development and staffing of new agencies that would alleviate these problems or toward the revamping of old agencies for the same purpose. Every crisis that arose presented an opportunity. Every session of the *Majlis* (Parliament) presented opportunities.

In order to prepare students to cope with the social problems defined as representing a high priority, specific new courses were established in the curriculum. Thus, the interest in family planning led to courses such as Population Studies, and Dynamics of Population Growth and Family Planning. The interest in rural-to-urban migration resulted in courses such as Economic Demography, and Urban and Rural Community Development. The concern about rights of women led to specific content on that subject in courses such as Seminars on Family, Child, Youth and Workers' Welfare; Law and Social Welfare; and Laws Affecting Children, Youth and Family. The definition of illiteracy as a pressing social problem led to a stress on educational approaches in such courses as Social Welfare and Services, Introduction to Social Work Methods, Economic and Social Changes in Iran. Concern with poor diet and nutrition led to a course on Nutrition, including planning the family diet and budgeting.

A complete list of courses for the first two years, last two undergraduate years, and Masters program is provided in Appendix A. It should be noted that Persian colleges and universities, specifically including professional schools, do not require as extensive liberal arts offerings as is the case in many other nations. The courses listed as required in Appendix A therefore comprise a fairly complete curriculum with electives added only under special circumstances.

THE BOARD OF TRUSTEES

The Teheran School of Social Work became one of the first institutions of higher learning to be organized under an independent board of trustees. This action established a pattern which has been followed by other educational institutions in Iran.

The chief functions of the board of trustees have been, throughout its existence, fund-raising as well as policy-making. In the former capacity, the board secures funds from governmental as well as private philanthropic sources for buildings, equipment,

additional personnel, and the many other requirements of a rapidly expanding school. In addition to its fund-raising and public relations duties, the board has helped the School in passing laws
significant to social welfare and in establishing new programs and
services. The members of the board have, therefore, been selected
from the standpoint of their potential influence on policy-making
as well as their involvement in the employment of social work
personnel. The board has a constitutional requirement that it
meet quarterly, but it may meet more often as the need arises.

The Minister of Court continues to serve as chairman of the
board. Other board members include the following: Director of
the Pahlavi Foundation, Minister of Science and Higher Education,[18] Minister of Social Welfare, Minister of Labor and Social
Affairs, Minister of Health, Minister of Finance, Minister of Information, Chancellor of Teheran University, Mayor of Teheran,
Director of the Red Lion and Sun Society, Director of the Imperial Organization for Social Services, Chairman of the Chamber
of Commerce and Industries, Director of the School of Social
Work, and two representatives of the community nominated by
the Director of the School of Social Work and approved by the
board of trustees.

The patronage and interest of Queen Farah in social welfare
has set the stage for a high degree of interest on the part of these
board members in expanding social work education and developing the social services in Iran. Moreover, the Shah has repeatedly
stressed the need to curtail population growth and to prepare
rural migrants to fit into urban, industrial life. The Shah gave the
School his backing from the beginning, since its objectives so
clearly coincided with his plan to raise the standard of living of
the people and to promote a greater degree of social justice.[19] He
was among the first to contribute funds to the School, and has
consistently retained a strong interest. The Queen has been very
interested in the education of social workers as well as in encouraging the utilization of social workers in family planning
clinics, community welfare centers, and children's institutions.
Each time the Shah or Queen open or visit children's institutions, hospitals, or other welfare agencies, an early question often
asked is, "Where is your social worker?" If the agency does not

have a social worker, its director is likely to arrange soon for one. The backing of the royal family has been supplemented by the support of the Minister of Court and other board members.

In brief, a combination of humanitarian and pragmatic considerations has paved the way for cabinet ministers and other high officials to assume a greater share of leadership in social work and social work education than would be the case in a country whose leaders had different goals and concerns. True enough, those social services rather closely related to population control, expanding the pool of trained workers, and easing the transition from rural to urban life have received a high priority in the minds of the leadership, so that other social problems such as mental illness, crime, and child neglect have perhaps received somewhat less attention. But it is anticipated that the leadership of Iran will move more readily toward the resolution of these problems, as well as toward a more developmental view of social welfare, after immediate and critical social problems are faced.

In any case, the Iran experience seems to indicate that leadership can be won over to support social work and social work education if facts are carefully gathered, if relevance to national goals and aspirations (such as the White Revolution) are clearly demonstrated, if recommendations are presented fairly and with conviction, and if social workers have perseverance and courage. Advocates and supportive groups, of course, need to be carefully cultivated, the press and other media kept informed, and contact maintained with all power groups in the society.

RELATIONSHIP WITH THE FAMILY PLANNING ASSOCIATION OF IRAN AND THE COMMUNITY WELFARE CENTER OF IRAN

Following its first field experiences in 1958, the School realized that welfare work in Iran could not be successful if family planning were not among the services offered. This realization followed from the increasing pressure of population growth on rising standards, which threatened to wipe out the results of higher income, increased industrial employment, and better living conditions. But perhaps even more dramatic was the impact on early students of being overwhelmed by the physical crowding and the sheer numbers of people. The streets were almost impassable, being so full of children who had nowhere else to play. Experience after experience reinforced the conclusion that there were too many people for the few available facilities. Economic, health, housing and educational resources to meet the needs of all these people were simply lacking. The students reported seeing homes in which families with ten or more children lived in one room about ten feet square, and with only one small pot of food to serve the entire family. One early student recalls such a family in which the last two of eleven children had been twins. Since there was literally no room for them, they had been placed on the *korsi* (the local heating system).

Sixty students might be squeezed into a tiny classroom. Social workers saw 150 children waiting to get into a class with a capacity for 25. A hospital with 100 beds might have as many as 500 people in line to be admitted. Playgrounds sometimes had two swings, with 50 children awaiting turns. Rooming houses were bursting at the seams. Streets were swarming.

Thus, in 1958, the School cooperated in the establishment of the Family Planning Association of Iran. The Association continues to work in close liaison with the School, and its headquarters are located on the School's campus.

The policy of the School has been to acquaint the total student body with the philosophy of family planning and to provide all students with at least an observation experience. Courses in the dynamics of population growth and family planning, and in human sexuality and sex education, support the emphasis placed on family planning at the School.

Over a third of the students have had their field placements in Family Planning Association clinics, ten of which are located in Teheran and eleven in the provinces. (Details of the FPA clinics are given in Chapter V.) Over 50 student research projects have been carried out in the area of population and family planning. Eight of 29 graduate students elected to do their research in some aspect of population and family planning in 1971–1972, and the percentage was higher in 1972–1973. In the 1972 academic year, eight of 63 fourth-year undergraduate students undertook research projects on family planning or related topics.

In addition to the establishment of family planning services, it was obvious that a need of equal importance was the development of services to work with people who had migrated from rural to urban areas and who needed help in adjusting to the new environment. The School, therefore, recognized the need for new structures that would combine a variety of service programs for individuals, families, groups and neighborhoods, particularly in overcrowed urban areas serving the rural migratory population. While providing social welfare services, these structures would also offer opportunities for field instruction. The result was the establishment of the Community Welfare Center of Iran, in which the School played a leading role. These centers offer a range of services including day care, maternal and child health programs, group programs for youth, literacy and vocational training, and community organization programs in addition to casework and group work. (The activities of the Community Welfare Center are described at length in Chapter VI). About one-third of the students have been placed in community welfare centers for field instruction and more than 45 graduates, faculty and students were working in the 22 centers in operation in early 1974.

OBJECTIVES OF THE SCHOOL

1. To provide professional education.

2. To strengthen and extend the scope of social work agencies in Iran through staff guidance and training. Also to encourage social work education in other parts of the country.

3. To carry on research into social problems and into the ways of dealing with such problems, and to evaluate the effectiveness of new social work methods.

4. To develop new techniques for the prevention and treatment of social problems.

5. To inform society about the nature of the social workers' task and to interpret their role in the modern community; and to convey the importance of professional education and technical skills in social work practice.

PROGRAM OF STUDY

Professional education in any field should be directly related to the requirements of the work which will be performed upon completion of training. The principal objective of the programs offered by the School of Social Work is to educate social workers who, having acquired the necessary knowldege and skill, will be equipped to undertake professional duties and apply their theoretical knowledge in practice, not only through direct service but also through interpretation of their programs and needs to the public.

The programs have been developed in accordance with international principles of social work and educational standards. At the same time an effort has been made to adapt them to meet the needs of Iran, its traditions, its current economic and social conditions, and its educational possibilities. Since the School was opened at the beginning of the recent period of Iran's development, efforts have been made to prepare social workers to assist in the attainment of these development goals, as they related to social welfare. The diploma, B.A. and M.A. programs include both theoretical and practical instruction.

Theoretical instruction is in five major areas:

1. Human behavior and the social environment.

Attention is given to the reciprocal relationship between the individual, including his physical, intellectual, emotional and social development and functioning, and the socio-cultural, political and economic environment. The student should understand the development of the individual as a social being, the motives that underline behavior, and the responses which might be expected at different stages of development and in differing environmental situations. The student should also be aware of the significance for human development of social institutions and organizations, including the family, peer groups, and economic and political institutions.

2. *Social welfare policy and services.*

The stress is on the application of knowledge from the social and behavioral sciences to the understanding of social problems, and to the prevention and control of social problems as well as for the enhancement of social functioning. The student is expected to understand the origin of social problems in urbanization, industrialization, and social change, and should be able to assess current social policies and services and to plan more effective policies and services.

3. *Human experience from an historical and philosophical perspective.*

Philosophy, the arts and literature can make students aware of man's cultural heritage and thereby give insights into human behavior.

4. *Problem-solving methods.*

The subjects studied are logic, scientific methods and mathematics.

5. *Social work principles and methods.*

There are three traditional methods of social work intervention: individual casework, group work and community work. Students learn both the unique and the common factors in these methods as well as the fundamental underlying principles which must be followed in their work. In addition, students are taught the value and principles of social structural change, legislative process, organizational change, administration, and social action.

The diploma, B.A. and M.A. programs all cover these core topics, but each program is reviewed annually and arranged to meet the needs of the students concerned as well as the needs of the different sections of the community.

FIELD INSTRUCTION

Field instruction enables students to relate theory to practice by applying classroom theories to benefit clients and alleviate social problems. The students are therefore taught to select the appropriate methods to meet the needs of the client and are trained in the use of individual, group and community methods as well as in organizational change, social action, social structural change, administration and research. Field placements were also developed with the intention of making social workers instruments of social change in the development of the country, e. g., field placements in rural areas. The training programs are arranged to give adequate learning opportunities not only in theory but also in practical experience of field instruction agencies. As the student's knowledge of field work practice increases year by year, correspondingly higher standards are set by field work instructors.

Instructors are assigned by the School to guide the students and to improve the service they give to their clients. They are selected on the basis of their background and experience in different agencies and are therefore able to use their own experiences as teaching aids for the students.

The instructors' duties are not limited to individual field instruction, but also include weekly consultative meetings with groups of students. During these meetings, the students' treatment plans are evaluated and discussed, with the instructor participating as a group member as well as a guide. Consequently, the student can effect his plan with a deeper insight into both the client and himself. By learning to recognize his own faults and weaknesses, the student is given the opportunity of evaluating more fully his own feelings and reactions and those of the client. These sessions also enable the instructors to remain current with new thinking and ideas in social work.

The School has taken great care in the choice of the field instruction agencies to be used for the students' placements. The criteria for selection have been the learning opportunities offered and the degree of compatibility between the principles, objectives and practice of social work and the policy of the agency. Those agencies which have been selected include child centers, prisons, education centers, health agencies such as mental hospitals and hospitals for drug addicts, factories, community welfare centers, Family Planning Association clinics, and rural villages. During their placement, students have the same responsibilities as full-time staff and must follow the agency's regulations and policy.

THE RESEARCH GROUP

In addition to theoretical work and field instruction, the School provides opportunities for students to develop new methods of tackling social problems by means of study and research. They are then able to attempt new approaches and plan new services. The results of the students' experimental work are assessed by the research faculty and, if thought to be of value, they are later implemented in social programs. The School has two staff members responsible for instruction in research, one at the undergraduate level and one at the graduate level, who guide the work that is carried out. The research faculty comprises an experimental research group, established for the purposes of teaching and increasing knowledge. The School has tried to enforce the use of scientific methods and the work carried out could therefore be considered original research. The research group is in close contact with policy-makers, field instructors, researchers and statisticians, and it is accepted that there should be maximum cooperation among all forces. Government and private agencies have commissioned a number of research projects for the student group to carry out. One of the most significant studies accomplished by the Teheran School of Social Work was a pioneer analysis of prostitution for the Ministry of Interior and the City of Teheran. Examples of other important research projects carried out include:
(1) A study of the reasons for divorce in Teheran, involving an inquiry directed at families coming to the divorce court. (2) A survey of induced or medical abortion in Farah and Saleh Hospitals in Teheran. (3) A survey of the health, economic status, nutrition, social problems and family problems of children hospitalized at Reza Pahlavi Hospital in Teheran. (4) A study of the reasons why handicapped persons do not use the prosthetic appliances they receive at the Rehabilitation Center in Teheran. (5) A survey of the causes of addiction among prostitutes in the red-light district of Teheran. (6) A survey of the causes of sui-

cide among youths between the ages of 15 and 25, conducted in a Teheran hospital. (7) Causes of opium addiction and its short and long-term effects. (8) A survey of the problems of children of women in the red-light district of Teheran. (9) Financial, social and emotional effects on children who have lost their parents. (10) An evaluation of the program of a vocational school for teenagers at Karadj.

VOLUNTEERS

Volunteers have played a valuable role in the development and provision of social services and the School has always supported such activities. The School has therefore established professional classes and short courses for the education and training of volunteers. Through such courses volunteers are familiarized with the agencies in which they work; they gain knowledge not only of the agencies' functions and procedures, but also of the type of help that is required and what they themselves can offer. Volunteers are presently active in a hospital for addicts, in the family planning program, the community welfare centers, and in the School itself.

SOCIAL LEGISLATION AND SOCIAL ACTION

The Teheran School of Social Work has, throughout its history, taken an active role in social action, social planning, social legislation, and social policy. For example, the School was a major force in the enactment of a new Juvenile Court Act by the Iranian Parliament *(Majlis)*, as well as the enactment of more progressive legislation affecting women's rights, child welfare, and family relations.

The process used in this activity includes a close relationship with the Ministries, which draft much of the legislation, and with members of Parliament, who consider the proposed legislation. The Director of the School discusses legislation regularly with members of the Board of Trustees, with the Minister of Court, and with Parliament members who are particularly interested in social legislation.

A close and continuing relationship is maintained with Plan

and Budget Organization, which often develops the planning upon which specific legislation is based.

Graduates of the School, students, and faculty members are also related to social legislation and planning, since they are often in a position to have some direct input as well as to keep the School aware of developments and trends.

Frequently, students have taken the lead in social action, such as reporting poor conditions in institutions and insisting that remedial measures be taken. Often in Iran people in all walks of life have opportunities to present grievances and recommendations by petition to the office of the Shah, Queen or Prime Minister, and at times students as well as clients have taken advantage of such opportunities to suggest ideas for more legislation or programs which in turn were referred to the Ministries and Parliament.

OTHER ACTIVITIES OF THE SCHOOL

Because the School has always believed that its role is not limited to teaching, training and research, it has accepted every opportunity of offering practical help in handling major social problems or meeting national emergencies. Some examples of what the School has done are as follows:

1. The School has taken part in rescue operations such as those following earthquakes, offering economic and social assistance to the victims. Students have gone to the earthquake areas and participated in such projects as the building of children's centers, the establishment of schools and high schools, counting of earthquake casualties and the provision of water, food, and other help to the villagers. Since 1958, the staff and students have helped in five major earthquakes.

2. The School cooperated with the Ministry of Health in 1970 to prevent a cholera epidemic.

3. A Family Aid Society was established in 1958 in cooperation with the National Vocational Center with the help of volunteers. The program is intended to meet the emergency needs of families and prevent begging. Social workers determine which families have the greatest need and to what extent

they should be helped. In 1970–1972, about 2,000 families were helped with the following forms of assistance:

a. The provision of financial help to meet daily expenses in the event of disaster emergencies.
b. The provision of capital to the head of a family to start a small business.
c. The purchase of medicines in order to assist with medical care.
d. Aid with school fees and clothing for school children.
e. The provision of tickets to those who live in the provinces in order that they may return to their homes.

The Family Aid Society was developed as a pilot project in the absence of any such program. The need for this kind of program on a national scale was later discussed with the government, which in 1973 took over the idea of the Family Aid Society and greatly expanded it.

4. For the first few years of its existence, the School concentrated on meeting the needs of its full-time students, but later, with the help of UNICEF, the School was able to provide some in-service training and education for the staff of social agencies. One program is a series of seminars for the staff of the community welfare centers. They have also trained staff for a rehabilitation center in Karadj, provided teacher training for centers run by the Women's Organization, and trained the housemothers in the municipal orphanage in Teheran. Most Teheran social agencies now look to the School to provide their staff with educational programs, and the School is trying to give as much help as possible.

5. The School is the Iranian representative of the International Social Service, an agency concerned with social welfare problems of an international nature, and particularly with the welfare problems of children where several countries may be involved as in child custody and adoption cases.

ISSUES AND PROBLEMS

A major problem at the Teheran School of Social Work, in common with schools in all developing countries, has been the overdependence on concepts, research and teaching materials from other countries, particularly in the West, and the resulting lack of sufficient indigenous study material. Various writers have stressed that social work education, while responsive to a universal framework, must take place within the social, cultural, economic, and political context of a particular country and be related to the needs of that country.[20] Although the Teheran School of Social Work has related itself to Persian needs in a Persian context, the shortage of written indigenous materials has led to the initial adoption of methods and approaches utilized in North American social work. As in other developing countries, methods, textbooks, illustrative case material, and concepts and techniques in general have been adapted from other countries, particularly the United States. Nagpaul and Shawky have pointed to similar problems in India and in Africa.[21]

Among the serious problems created by the heavy dependence on materials and concepts from other countries is an often uncritical acceptance of methods and concepts which may not really be applicable in the receiving country. Nagpaul, for example, has noted that social work education that maintains the traditional conceptions of working with individuals, groups and communities and is predicated on a philosophy of strengthening people's capacity to cope with their own problems, may not be relevant to Indian society and culture.[22]

The Teheran School of Social Work continues to examine critically the applicability of North American and European methods and concepts in Iran, as well as to develop a great deal more indigenous teaching material. Within the next decade, there should be extensive development of native Persian textbooks. Persian social work is giving attention to the social structure as well as problems at the individual and family level. Concentrated attention is being given to the development of Persian patterns of social work education and Persian patterns of manpower utilization.

A recent example of development of Persian teaching materials may be of interest. An anthology of Persian poems, folk tales and fables is being developed for use in first-year courses in Persian Composition as well as in Social Work Methods. The contents have been selected for their usefulness in illustrating various social work concepts. From these readings, students can recognize that the principles of social work have been a part of their heritage for centuries.

Students should be prepared to help in the future expansion of a network of social resources of importance to the Persian society, such as family planning and community welfare centers, which will tend toward the strengthening of a developmental and preventive approach to social welfare.[23]

Students should perhaps be purposefully recruited from rural areas of Iran, as more educational facilities are available to rural areas, to help with the very serious issue of encouraging the development of social services in rural areas. Although many of them may still elect to remain in Teheran, some of those recruited from rural areas may want to return after graduation.

Future Directions of the School

The Teheran School of Social Work is the first and, in 1974, still the only school of its type in Iran. It is also the only school of social work in the region with a full two-year graduate program. Several possibilities exist for future development.

1. It will probably serve as the prototype for additional schools of social work to be developed in provincial capitals in Iran, as more educational facilities are developed in the provinces. This step would seem to be a logical one to help develop the manpower needed to cope with social changes occurring as a result of the White Revolution.

2. It will expand and strengthen the quality of instruction, esspecially in research, policy, and methods of intervention. The curriculum will gradually place greater stress on group work, community organization and development, organizational change, societal change, policy and program development, and legislative action, although individual and family casework will still be taught.

3. In the 1980s it has a strong likelihood of serving as a regional center for the preparation of advanced students in social work as well as training in family planning at various levels,

with the help of the United Nations, International Planned Parenthood Federation, and other international agencies.

4. A much stronger research, demonstration, and experimentation center may be developed as more personnel with doctoral degrees join the faculty. Much of this research and demonstration might logically involve the social aspects of family planning, the work of community welfare centers, social policy formulation and planning at the national level, and community development.

5. Writers and leaders in social welfare such as Julia Henderson, long associated with the United Nations and now with the International Planned Parenthood Federation, have stressed the vital role that private voluntary schools and agencies can play in social policy evaluation and formulation. In addition to the research role in policy evaluation and formulation outlined above, it is likely that the Teheran School of Social Work will develop a social policy center which will have as its functions the analysis of social welfare policies, in conjunction with its research center, and the systematic formulation of alternative policies to resolve the nation's social problems. The work would be done in close collaboration with Plan and Budget Organization and the results and recommendations would be turned over to appropriate government ministries for review and possible implementation. This would follow the well-established pattern in such advanced countries as Britain, France, the Netherlands, Sweden and the United States.

Chart I
GROWTH OF THE STUDENT BODY *

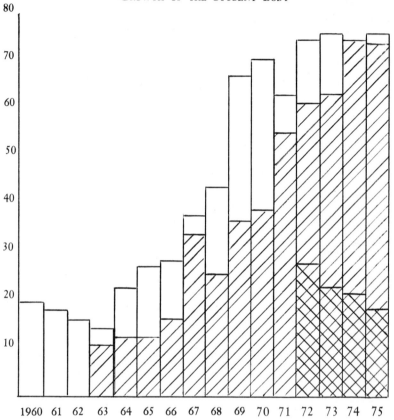

Graduates of two-year diploma course ☐

Graduates of baccalaureate program ▨

Students enrolled in Master's program ▧

* The School opened in 1958 and graduated its first class two years later.

Chart II
EMPLOYMENT OF TEHERAN SCHOOL OF SOCIAL WORK GRADUATES

Agency	%	
Medical settings: mental hospitals, narcotics hospital and insurance hospitals.	20	(74)*
Family planning: Ministry of Health, Family Planning Association of Iran.	10.5	(38)
Community development and rural welfare.	9.5	(34)
Ministry of Labor and Rehabilitation Center.	7.5	(27)
Ministry of Justice, Ministry of Finance, Ministry of Interior and Municipality.	8	(29)
Plan Organization, oil industry, radio and television, statistics center, banks, factories, labor welfare.	8	(29)
Student agencies: student welfare, universities and schools of higher education.	7	(23)
Orphanages, agencies dealing with children and youth centers.	5	(17)
Community welfare centers.	3	(11)
Ministry of Court, Office of Her Imperial Majesty, Prime Ministry.	2	(8)
Teheran School of Social Work, education of social workers	2	(7)
Studying abroad.	7.5	(27)
Currently not in practice.	10	(35)
		(363)

*Number in parenthesis indicates actual number of graduates.

A Social Worker as
Agent of Social Change

The folowing chapter specifically discusses the role of the director of the Teheran School of Social Work, Sattareh Farman-Farmaian, in helping to carry out some of the changes in social institutions required by the White Revolution.

X The Role of the Director of the Teheran School of Social Work in Implementing the Social Aspects of the White Revolution

The early history of social work in England and the United States involved leadership by upper class or upper middle class individuals who perceived the need for new social policies and social services and proceeded to meet those needs through their own crusading or philanthropic efforts.[1] Sometimes called a "Lady Bountiful" period, this early stage in the history of social work saw decisions being made by humanitarian, forceful, and determined men and women who were often wealthy and influential enough to have a direct impact on social policy. In England, one thinks of the Webbs, particularly Beatrice Webb, as a prototype of the reformer and crusader.[2] In the United States, Jane Addams established one of the earliest settlement houses in Chicago, was influential in the passage of a number of early examples of social legislation, and served as a leader in social action and community organization. Dorothea Dix almost singlehandedly convinced most of the legislators in the mid-1800s to establish hospitals for mentally ill.

The logic behind this early stage in social work is clear; at the time, no formal institutions, organizations, or other frameworks existed to assume leadership in social policy and social services. Able individuals with money, friends, social positions, or other avenues to power came forward to take the first steps in social legislation and policy, usually acting at some point to help create the institutions or organizations that later assumed more formal and institutionalized roles in social policy.

Social work and social legislation in Iran has followed a similar pattern. As indicated in Chapter IX, a variety of social agencies were established in the 1940s and 1950s, as it became clear that industrialization and urbanization were creating social problems with which the traditional social order could not adequately cope. These agencies were established under the leadership of upper class individuals and families, including the Shah's sisters and other members of the royal family, with the status and financial resources to initiate social change. In 1958, Miss Sattareh Farman-Farmaian was invited to make a specific proposal to establish a school of social work in Iran, in recognition of the need to have an educational facility in the country to prepare personnel for the increasing number of public and private social agencies. Miss Farman-Farmaian received the invitation because she was the first professionally qualified Iranian.[3] She has served as a professional in a transition period from a "Lady Bountiful" period.

Her professional qualifications not only included a Master's degree in social work, but, from 1954 to 1958, she was a United Nations social welfare advisor to the Government of Iraq. Three years after she accompanied Mr. Arthur Altmayer on a United Nations study in Iran in 1955 (see Chapter IX), Mr. Abol Hassan Ebtahaj, who was then head of Plan Organization, came to Baghdad and invited Miss Farman-Farmaian to come to Iran to study the social welfare institutions and to work for the Plan Organization. On this visit, in April 1958, she agreed to return to Iran under one condition: that she be allowed to establish a school to develop qualified manpower for the Persian social welfare agencies. Plan Organization accepted her condition. From both the initial investigation in 1955 and her discoveries upon returning to Iran, she felt that the first priority was to train personnel to man the social welfare agencies.

After her proposal was accepted and as she initiated and continued the development of the Teheran School of Social Work, Miss Farman-Farmaian perceived the need for new legislation:

to extend the rights of women in a strongly male-dominated society, to establish a juvenile court system that could provide more adequately for the rights and needs of children, and to modernize the divorce laws. In general, she sought to develop a statutory commitment to social justice for women, children, rural migrants to the cities, beggars, prostitutes, the physically handicapped, the mentally ill and retarded, and other groups in need of help.

In the early years of the school's operation, Miss Farman-Farmaian verified the observation made during the period as a United Nations consultant that numerous families in developing countries could not cope with their problems because they had too many children. The verification occurred in direct observation in the streets of South Teheran where the first groups of students were in field work. In her opinion during this early year, successful work with the families there was obviously impeded by family size. Fairly soon afterwards she began to develop the organization later known as the Family Planning Association of Iran.

Still later she perceived a need for multipurpose social agencies that would help to prepare rural immigrants for urban living, and strongly supported the establishment and operation of the Community Welfare Center in Iran.

Gradually, the three ventures became housed in the same complex in Teheran, with Miss Farman-Farmaian as head of all three. It should be noted that all three agencies (the Teheran School of Social Work, the Family Planning Association of Iran, and the Community Welfare Center of Iran) are all private, nongovernmental agencies with their own boards, who elected Miss Farman-Farmaian as chairman (FPA and CWC) or appointed her as director (Teheran School of Social Work). It should be further noted that these agencies came into existence gradually because of existing and perceived needs, not because of a preconceived grand plan. The Family Planning Association and the Community Welfare Center began with no real physical existence as agencies, consisting simply of people doing things of concern and interest to the school. These people were initially faculty, students, and friends of the School. CWC began on a small scale from field-work pilot projects, not actually becoming a formal organization until 1970. The FPA was also an informal group until the Queen visited Javadieh Community Welfare Center in 1966 and asked what the center needed. At the time, the family planning "clinic" consisted of a single room. The Queen gave money to establish a real clinic attached to the Javadieh Center.

The arrangement of three agencies, howveer, after it did evolve, was a development familiar to other social work pioneers such as Jane Addams which gave Miss Farman-Farmaian a unique opportunity to interrelate programs. Thus, social work students receive much of the field experience in family-planning clinics and community welfare centers. The family-planning clinics are typically located in the community welfare centers. Social work staff members for the family-planning clinics and community welfare centers are largely drawn from the School's graduates. Other staff members are drawn from the community. Some staff members of the Family Planning Association and the Community Welfare Center also serve as field work supervisors and lecturers at the Teheran School of Social Work. In short, the decisions, policies, personnel, and programs of the three organizations are now intertwined, with Miss Farman-Farmaian directing all three and subject to the policies established by respective controlling boards, although she only receives one salary. Her positions with the FPA and CWC are honorary. This arrangement has helped to make it possible for the three organizations to get adequate funding and government backing.

In the development of the three programs, Miss Farman-Farmaian has received the support both of the government and of the Royal Family, especially the Queen. After the programs proved themselves, she has been able to reach top policy-makers as well as philanthropists when any of the organizations has had a serious need for funds.

In a real sense, all three organizations have filled the classical role of the private agency in the United States, i. e., that of initial exploration, experimentation, and demonstration. Further, the three organizations can be perceived as meeting the problems of the country at that time: 1) No trained manpower; 2) Too many children in low income groups; 3) A need for a self-help method. These factors were preeminent in the establishment and organization of the various agencies. The government has closely followed the progress of three programs, for example, by establishing an undersecretary in charge of family planning in the Ministry of Health and tripling the government support of the Family Planning Association in 1974, both steps being taken in recognition of the success of FPA.

Now, on all sides in Iran, we see developments that portend the social work profession of the future and many of the developments were initiated or shared in by Miss Farman-Farmaian. The Iranian Association of Social Workers was formed in 1961, aimed at furthering the interests of the profession. There has been an expansion of most of the various social welfare programs. Plan Organization will provide money to construct forty family welfare centers each year for the next five years, with the programming, staffing, and operating of them being the responsibility of the Community Welfare Center of Iran. Plan Organization sets development goals and provides funds for both government and private agencies in Iran, so that there is a close partnership between the public and private sector.

In the latest plan, the budget of the Teheran School of Social Work has been doubled and a million dollars has been allocated for the expansion of the physical plant. Broader programs of social insurance, rural development, housing and urban renewal, public health and education, aimed at a more institutional or developmental approach to social welfare, will gradually supplant the earlier and urgent remedial or residual programs initiated in the 1960s, and in any case, the latter will probably take on more institutional or developmental characteristics.[4]

This glimpse at the future, however, does not minimize the great importance of the earlier programs. They help to open a number of doors and to start a number of new services in Iran. Several questions may be of interest to other developing countries, to their social workers, and to the faculties of their schools. How has Miss Farman-Farmaian managed to obtain the support of the Royal Family and government and private sources? Why did she select the particular residual services, such as the community welfare centers, to focus upon? Is she thoughtfully preparing for a

transition to institutional or developmental services? Are future
social welfare leaders being prepared to replace her?

*How has Miss Farman-Farmaian managed to obtain the support
of Royal Family and other government and private sources?* She
indicates that she has received their support because they saw in
her someone who perceived the problems, did something about
them, did not demand payment or reward, and was not pushing
herself or her spouse for position or power. She has never gone
to the government for funds until she has demonstrated what
could be done. In short, the securing of support from the Royal
Family and other members of the government has been through
perception and effort, and not simply a matter of access through
her position as a member of an upper class family.

As she has demonstrated her ability to develop viable and relevant social welfare programs as well as a strong and effective
school of social work, the Queen, the Queen's mother, the Prime
Minister, the Minister of Court, and a number of other ministers
and vice-ministers have offered support and encouragement. Since
she has studied carefully the social dimensions and consequences
of the White Revolution, she has been given opportunities to
make recommendations regarding social policies and social legislation affecting women's rights, family planning, services to children, and social services to families.

The Queen has personally visited the Teheran School of Social
Work and some of the welfare centers, and has received direct
information about the programs on these occasions. The Shah
has never visited the School although he is very interested in it
and gives a regular monthly donation to it.

Miss Farman-Farmaian also maintains contacts directly with
influential members of the Majlis (Parliament), wealthy and influential businessmen and philanthropists, university officials, leading professionals, and others.

One of her important assets is that she has maintained, as have
other important social and government administrators, very close
relationships with such international bodies as the United Nations,
the International Planned Parenthood Federation, the International Association of Schools of Social Work, and a variety of
other groups. She is frequently invited to serve on boards of di-

rectors of these international groups, to give speeches at their conferences, to publish papers in their journals, and to function as advisor or consultant to their activities. And, by a kind of reciprocal benefit, these international bodies are particularly interested in having her as officer, speaker, and consultant, precisely because she has been able to experiment in various social service programs in Iran.

One secret of her success has been her ability to obtain funding from individual philanthropists as well as from various foundations, groups, and individuals. Thus, the government has not had to be really committed until the demonstration or experiment has shown its value. She has been able to pioneer in programs that fit into the goals and aims of the White Revolution, which the government ministries were later able to adapt and revise for nationwide application. The government benefits, in that risk and cost are minimized. The government ministries have a chance to see how new programs work before mass utilization plans are firmed up. She has the satisfaction of pioneering at the national level while maintaining a prestigious relationship with international organizations.

The process of pioneering, demonstrating, testing, and final institutionalization may be illustrated by a review of a few of the services and programs which Miss Farman-Farmaian initiated and the ministries later adopted as part of a national development program. For example, when she established the family planning clinics in Iran, they were largely under social work leadership and a part of a total social welfare system. But as the Ministry of Health has shared responsibility for the nationwide program, the medical profession has exercised a degree of control. The Fifth Development Plan reviews the need for reduction of the annual rate of growth of population to 2.6 per cent by the end of the Fifth Plan and concludes: "It is expected that the Fifth Plan's *health system* will expand to enable this target to be met."[5]

A balance of interests has evolved, in which the Ministry of Health carries responsibility for family-planning policy but a number of private agencies help carry out the policy. The primary job of the FPA is education and motivation, whereas the Ministry of Health is responsible for overall policy and the establishment of clinics and the training of medical personnel. Miss Farman-Farmaian believes that family planning can be successful if it is integrated with the social welfare system in a pattern of close working relationships with the Ministry of Health clinics.

Similarly, Miss Farman-Farmaian has heavily stressed day care to pre-school children, with a focus on nutritional programs and nutritional education to mothers. When this program was considered appropriate for national coverage, the Ministries of Education and Health have taken primary responsibility, although Miss Farman-Farmaian's initial programs were under social welfare leadership. The Fifth Plan notes that "Meals will be provided for all children in rural kindergartens (138,000 at the end of the Plan period) and for needy children in urban kindergartens (220,-000 at the end of the Plan period) . . . The Ministry of Health will be responsible for carrying out a programme of educating the public in nutritional principles . . ."[6] The government, through various ministries, is responsible for the hot lunch program, and it now extends through primary and secondary schools.

Another example of changes is in the area of social welfare manpower training. Miss Farman-Farmaian naturally has looked to the Teheran School of Social Work as the vehicle for manpower training for social welfare. The Fifth Plan, however, after reviewing a number of welfare needs, lists manpower objectives as including: "to train 250 experts in various categories of welfare services by changing the curricula of related sciences such as sociology, psychology, and educational science; to train 100 social planning experts at the postgraduate level; to provide a new course for training child instructors with a capacity of 100 persons and expand the existing institute to train 600 child instructors at the postsecondary level; to provide short-term training courses in cooperation with executive agencies in order to train 650 assistant child instructors; to create a new inservice and preservice training unit for the existing staff of social and public welfare organizations as well as for new recruits; and to provide training for about 1,200 executives of public welfare organizations."[7] Most of these projected training programs would appear to be located outside the Teheran School of Social Work. The only one that is clearly within the School's program is the annual preparation of 60 social workers. However, the Fifth Plan was revised with the unexpected increase in oil revenues in 1974. The new Fifth Plan includes the training of more manpower for social services and social welfare agencies at all levels and has rebudgeted the Teheran School of Social Work to graduate 100 social workers a year.

Why did she select the particular residual services, such as the community welfare centers, to focus upon? Miss Farman-Farmaian's graduate social work education was at the University of Southern California School of Social Work during the 1950's. As in all U. S. schools of social work during that period, the primary focus was on casework services of an ameliorative, remedial, or residual nature. It should be noted that Miss Farman-Farmaian majored in community organization and had only one course in casework theory. Moreover, she came in contact with a number of more concrete services while a consultant with the United Nations, including stress on nutrition, day care services, and, in particular, the combination of many services to families and children under one roof. She became aware of the need for more comprehensive services aimed at altering life styles, customs, traditions, and social institutions.

It seems clear that when the new Teheran School of Social Work was called upon to aid victims of floods and hurricanes, Miss Farman-Farmaian quickly saw the need for day care, vocational training, casework services, and related services to needy families. It seemed most efficient, both to her and to the philanthropists she approached for funds, to combine and integrate these services into one agency structure.

In any case, the social work literature of the 1950s was full of references to the need for multipurpose social agencies, in order to eliminate duplication of services, to cut costs, to avoid gaps in services, to provide for maximum utilization of professional staff, and to curtail the serious loss of clients involved in the referral process. While developed countries with established agencies had bureaucratic barriers to development of multipurpose agencies, a developing country like Iran could fairly easily start out with such agencies from the very beginning.

While essentially residual, in the sense that all the services were aimed basically at low-income families with many children, largely migrants to the cities, the services have preventive as well as rehabilitative ingredients. For example, from the outset a strong emphasis was placed on educational activities, self-help and vocational training.

She has been quite willing to adapt to the international interests in community development, physical needs of people, and stress on education and vocational training, and she has increasingly altered the curriculum from a psychoanalytically-oriented case-work model (utilized at the outset when foreigners—UN advisors and Fulbright fellows—taught methods) to one in which all intervention methods are taught.

She seems, on the whole, willing to allow faculty, students, and consultants to move in other than direct-service directions. For example, the author of this book supervised a research project of a graduate student at the Teheran School of Social Work whose interests were primarily of a political, developmental, and planning nature. He had little real interest in casework or other direct services.

As a fairly clear example of the direction in which both the Iranian social services system and Miss Farman-Farmaian were moving in 1974, it is instructive to examine the new law to establish a separate Ministry of Social Welfare, passed by the Majlis on July 29, 1974. She was a leading advocate of the new law.

The Ministry of Social Welfare was created with the following functions, which are clearly a mixture of the institutional or developmental approaches to Social Welfare with the residual or remedial:

a. Provision of universal medical care and medical insurance.
b. Provision of universal social security, e. g., socal insurance and aid to the indigent and the needy.
c. Provision of welfare services for all age groups, including family welfare centers, day-care centers, orphanages, youth facilities, and homes for the aged.
d. Treatment and rehabilitation of the physically, socially, and mentally handicapped. Treatment and rehabilitation of addicts and alcoholics.
e. Supervision of all welfare agencies, guidance and creation of

uniform standards, and assistance in manpower training.
  f. Participation in international organizations and conferences concerned with the problems outlined above.
  g. Coverage of all other welfare needs that might arise.
Note: Provision of these services in the villages is to be undertaken by the Ministry of Cooperatives and Rural Affairs.

Are future social welfare leaders being prepared to replace her?
It is fair to say that the Teheran School of Social Work is not the only facility preparing future leaders for social welfare in Iran. However, the Teheran School of Social Work has placed about 650 social workers in government agencies, social welfare agencies, ministries, and factories. They act as assistants to governors and mayors, they rank as high as director-generals in government agencies. Approximately 150 students have been sent abroad for further training. All the Teheran Community Welfare Centers and most of the Provincial Centers are now headed by graduate social workers.

In all, it appears that both the Teheran School of Social Work and the other programs are preparing leaders to continue and expand Miss Farman-Farmaian's work. These leaders may be less individualistic and most institutionally-centered in their approaches, but may also be less residual and increasingly developmental in the services they espouse and expand.

PART D

Conclusion and Future Prospects

Chapter XI highlights some of the probable future directions of the White Revolution and of the Teheran School of Social Work. Although not specifically a summary, the chapter does in part reemphasize some of the main threads in the foregoing chapters. But its main thrust is one of prediction, risky as this may be in an uncertain world with so many imponderables and unknowns.

In a sense, the chapter also tries to tie together the three main content areas of the book: the White Revolution; the Teheran School of Social Work particularly as it relates to the White Revolution; and the Director of the Teheran School of Social Work, Miss Sattareh Farman-Farmaian, as the architect of various social experiments in Iran related to the White Revolution.

XI   The Future Perspective

Problems and perspectives change over time, and it is to be expected that the White Revolution will change both its priorities and its character as consolidation of gains takes place and new needs emerge. Yet, it is likely that the overall purposes of social justice and redistribution of wealth will remain. The experience, in any case, in England and the Scandinavian countries has been that such overall purposes are easier to articulate than to realize.

The priorities for the next ten years include efforts to accelerate the development of low-cost housing, the expansion of education at all ages, the development of more vocational training opportunities, the expansion of the industrial base of the country, and other measures aimed at raising the level of education, health, welfare, and the standard of living of all segments of the nation. It is clear that the monarch of Iran is "committed to social change as well as to political longevity."[1]

By late 1974 the number of children in school had increased from four million in 1973 to six million.[2] Free education was extended in 1974 to all students from kindergarten to college, at a cost of 32 billion rials.[3] Free health care was extended to citizens in 1974, at a cost of 6.8 billion rials. This health program requires the training of 60,000 village health officers by the Imperial Social Service Organization, with the cooperation of the Ministry of Health.[4] Hospital units and physicians are being brought in from abroad to staff the new programs.[5] The health program will begin with simple services at the village level and build up to sophisticated clinics and hospitals in towns, provincial centers, and large cities.[6]

A gradual increase in democratic participation in decision-making can be anticipated, as the power of the traditional elite groups continues to decline. Zonis, as well as others, recognizes the broader base of recruitment to the bureaucracy.[7] And the Shah has amply demonstrated his political skill in changing his approach, style, and even his policies. As more Iranians become better educated, and as more Iranians demand a better level of living and more participation in decision-making, the Shah has stated that he will create a more democratic political structure. Political parties have emerged, and a Majlis with power and a degree of independence. Bill has pointed out that one of the more dramatic unintended effects of the White Revolution has been the expansion of the professional middle class.[8] Many peasants and workers are now moving into that class. Bayne has also recognized the future potential of the peasants as a political force.[9]

A major problem now is the shortage of qualified manpower for industry, the professions, and other sectors of the economy. A recent newspaper article notes that manpower is not available to staff the nationwide program of free education promised by the Government, or personnel to provide free health care, or manpower for other social and economic undertakings.[10] Already, hundreds of Russians are operating the new steel mill in Isfahan; U. S. military personnel are providing technical assistance to Iran's military build-up; French scientists and technicians are staffing the nuclear energy program; Indian and Pakistani physicians are providing medical care to rural areas in Iran; and Israeli experts are guiding farm cooperatives.[11]

The recent 400 percent increase in oil revenues has very recently resulted in the revision of the Fifth Development Plan. An accelerated development plan has been substituted, but serious shortages include manpower, food production, and water supply.

An accelerated thrust aimed at modernization of the rural areas of Iran will be a feature of planning in the decades ahead. Paydarfar stressed in 1967: "the data from the Iranian population showed that most of the Iranian provinces are in a very early stage of modernization and vary only slightly in degree of modernization."[12] Yet, the progress in the intervening decade has been considerable.

Rural development to lessen the gap between city and village had resulted by 1974 in the establishment of 1,002 houses of culture aimed at providing adult education to the rural population. The creation of 1,200 rural development zones, each including several villages, were providing medical, cultural, social, and rural industrial facilities to over 13,000 villages.[13] The Sixth Development Plan, beginning in 1978, will expand the number of these rural development zones. Rural development has also been accelerated by the formation of 2,793 rural cooperatives and 65 farm corporations. The former have 2,300,000 members. The rural cooperatives and farm corporations are aimed at improving traditional agricultural methods.

Another effort at rural and provincial development has been the government's encouragement of private firms, consulting engineers and contractors to locate in the provinces. This policy resulted from a recognition that redistribution of income will require more than programs of food subsidy, price control, and a graduated income tax.[14] Employment in the provinces will spread prosperity.[15] Redistribution of income will also require an extensive and long-term program of welfare services, according to the Director of the Plan and Budget Organization.[16] By 1980 or 1985, millions of peasants will have moved into the lower middle class in urban or urbanizing areas, and the need for better education, vocational training, health services, housing, cultural opportunities, social security, streets, parks, and employment will become an urgent and compelling one.[17]

THE FUTURE OF SOCIAL WORK EDUCATION

Social work education, in Iran as in other countries, must meet several responsibilities. Obviously, the most important of these responsibilities is to prepare men and women for changing professional careers, and this implies continual curriculum revision in the light of a new knowledge, new worldwide and national needs, and changing philosophical trends and values.

Even more fundamental is the responsibility for planning and carrying out research and experimentation, not only into knowledge areas basic to social work, but also into strategies and policies for the prevention and control of Iran's social problems and into strategies and policies for social development. Since social problems relate specifically to the economic and social structure of a particular society, it is becoming clear that a developing country cannot expect to import solutions and strategies from developed countries without adaptation. Such adaptation will require research and experimentation based on the context of the particular society.

These various functions and responsibilities are intertwined and closely related. Students can only learn the range of strategies for prevention and control of social problems and the strategies for social development if their teachers are prepared to teach a range of strategies, if the research and experimentation in these strategies has been successfully carried out, and if the curriculum is revised to facilitate such teaching and learning.

A school of social work, then, is a combination of laboratory, teaching-learning center, curriculum development center and research center in the areas of social problems management and social development.

A nation such as Iran has a right to expect schools of social work to fulfill these diverse but related responsibilities, and it has a corresponding obligation to furnish the resources, support and personnel to carry out these functions.

Schools of social work must be willing to encourage their faculty and students to participate in political, economic and educational processes if they are to meet these responsibilities. For example, the school must be willing to learn about, and become responsibly involved in, legislative and political processes if it is either to help fashion social policies and programs or if it is to *teach the process* of helping to fashion social policies and programs. This does not mean that the school, or its faculty or students, must identify with details of a particular party or program, but rather that it identify long-range and short-range social goals and then take mature and responsible steps toward the attainment of these goals.

The fearful traditionalist in social work education may wonder whether it is proper or fitting for a school of social work to identify social goals and attempt to realize them. But this is no more nor less an assumption of professional authority and responsibility than for the caseworker to take an active role in determining treatment goals for an individual client. The society, we may be sure, has its built-in defenses and resistances which will guarantee that no one profession can easily lead it "down the garden path," just as the individual has defenses and resistances. Modern societies all have a multiplicity of interest groups which balance and check each other. No society will, or can, move more rapidly toward specific goals of social development than the majority of its interest groups permits.

In the perspective of the foregoing observations, the experience of the Director of the Teheran School of Social Work in the social development of Iran has been an experiment in working with governmental, economic, and related institutions to move toward the attainment of the goals set by the White Revolution. This has included enlisting the cooperation of government officials and legislators to move the nation toward an acceptance of family planning, community development, and care of special groups such as retarded children. Laws have been passed to overhaul the juvenile court process and give more rights to women and children.

Vocational training programs have been established in the community welfare centers which have an impact on the economic institutions of the nation. In fact, the community welfare centers themselves represent a vehicle for preparing rural immigrants for urban life and hence are a combined social-economic-educational instrument. This appears to be at least one of the best ways to meet the shock of accelerated change as it is brought to bear on rural citizens moving into cities.

Such accomplishments as the Director of the Teheran School of Social Work has helped to bring about in Iran are not an exercise in magic. The usual requirements of hard work, continuation of interest, imagination and creativity are simply added to the tested ingredients of generic social work practice:

1. Develop priority needs for social development, preferably

in partnership with significant power groups or influential individuals.

2. Form teaching-service organizations such as the Family Planning Association of Iran and the Community Welfare Center of Iran which bring together the power groups and influential individuals to work on the priority needs which have been blocked out.

3. Accept and work closely with traditional power groups and influential individuals that do not initially favor meeting needs for social development or do not agree with social work methods but that can gradually be won over or influenced or whose successors can be won over or influenced.

4. Cooperate with the Chief of State, relevant government officials and ministries, the media and the public, with a two-way communication.

5. Maintain a willingness to revise goals and strategies in the light of changing needs and attitudes. A rigid set of goals can become a strait-jacket rather than a set of guidelines if flexibility and the need for periodic reassessment are not kept in mind.

6. Never lose sight of the ethical considerations that guide social work, including attention to the need to help forge a new philosophy and morality for people who often have lost traditional convictions under the impact of urbanization, westernization, and industrialization.[18]

The school of social work of the future can be a highly influential instrument for the planning and carrying out of socio-economic development in a nation or a region.

THE ROLE OF SOCIAL WORK EDUCATION IN FUTURE SOCIAL DEVELOPMENT IN IRAN

After seventeen years, the concept of social work has been accepted in Iran. There is a continuing demand for social workers in a variety of agencies. The need now is for more stress on quality, which in turn requires better teaching, more and better research, improved field instruction, more systematic curriculum development in social work education, more emphasis on advanced administration, more stress on the social work role in policy and planning, and more stress on evaluation of legislation.[19]

It is anticipated that future graduates of the Teheran School of Social Work will be better equipped to intervene and assist in a variety of roles and at many levels. The social worker of the future will need to be flexible enough and skilled enough to move into research roles, administrative roles, planning roles, legislative roles, educational roles and community development roles as the changing needs of Persian society may require. No less comprehensive a perspective of the role of social work education will serve to keep Persian social workers in a truly creative and significant relationship to changing social needs in Iran.

The Shah has repeatedly stressed his conviction that inequalities and injustices must be lessened if Iran is to become a viable society with economic democracy and social justice. Specifically, he states: "We are trying to do everything we can to expand the cooperatives and social welfare. We consider these to be basic essentials. We believe that a human being has the right to social welfare throughout his life, from the provision of education to sickness benefits, accident insurance, and old age pension.[20] Clearly, to achieve these goals in the next fifty years, assistance must be provided by a strong, progressive, and aggressive social work profession whose members have been prepared to help establish and maintain effective and workable social welfare laws, policies, and services. Other professions, such as education, medicine, law, and religion, will also play significant roles.

Another theme, noted in Chapter IX and mentioned briefly earlier in this chapter, is the need to develop a social work curriculum, social work methods, teaching materials, and social services specifically adapted to the Persian culture and the unique Persian needs. Iran has always, throughout its history, shown a capacity to adapt outside influences to its own culture and environment, and outside social work models have been adapted to the Persian context. A next order of business is clearly to develop Persian textbooks in social work, Persian teaching materials, Persian social work methods of practice, and to extend and augment the Persian system of social services that already has been developed.

Social work values throughout the world stress the worth and importance of the individual human being. Although methods and teaching materials need to be fashioned specifically for the Persian society, social work in Iran stands no less than other nations for the dignity and value of human life. Perhaps most important of all the social work contributions in Iran will be the effort to help forge a new philosophy for Persian citizens as old traditions and customs gradually change under the impact of urbanization and industrializiation. Without such a new philosophy, Iran might take over the relatively superficial material habits and preoccupations of the West while risking the loss of its values and social institutions.

Services have been concentrated in the urban sector, where income levels are already higher. This has meant that the overall distributive effect of social services to the rural areas has been limited. The Teheran School of Social Work may well need to develop in the decades ahead a particularly strong thrust toward development of a range of welfare services in provincial cities, towns and villages. In most of the developing countries, the key to social development lies in the rural areas.[21] The rapid migration to Teheran and other major cities can be expected to slow down as Teheran attains its maximum size, considering water availability, transportation factors and employment considerations, and as opportunities and needs grow in the rural areas. Iran is now upgrading the status of agriculture in the new budget and the new Fifth Plan and is providing more hope for the future for rural citizens. Also, the establishment of the new Ministry of Social Welfare and the passage of various laws regarding free medical care, free education, aid to the handicapped, aid to the indigent, and aid to widows and orphans, has expanded the government's responsibility for providing social services. These laws and the expanded governmental role will call for more social workers, and the school will be called upon to prepare a large number of personnel for both urban and rural areas.

Social workers will need to acquire a more sophisticated ability to modify social institutions, customs, and traditions as they move into more significant roles of social planning and community development in rural areas.

Appendix

The diploma, B.A. and M.A programs all cover these core topics, but each program is reviewed annually and arranged to meet the needs of the students concerned as well as the needs of different sections of the community.

The subjects covered in the diploma program (the first two years of study) are as follows:

1. Social welfare and services: social problems and planning to serve human needs.
2. Public health: physiology, physical growth and development, sex education and hygiene.
3. Developmental psychology: stages in the life cycle.
4: Introduction to psychology.
5. Population studies.
6. Nutrition, including planning the family diet and budgeting.
7. Principles of economics.
8. Logic as an introduction to social research.
9. Principles of sociology.
10. Social psychology, including social pathology and deviance.
11. Introduction to social work methods in casework, group work and community work.
12. Social welfare administration.
13. Law and social welfare.
14. Introduction to political science: Iran's governmental organization.

15. Introduction to statistics and research.
16. Mathematics for statistics.
17. Iran's history, philosophy and culture.
18. Persian composition.
19. English reading comprehension.

The subjects covered in the B.A. program (the second two years of study) are:
1. Political science and social welfare.
2. Analytical statistics, research methods, and preparation of a project.
3, 4, 5. Social casework, group work and community work taught as an integrated approach to social work intervention.
6. Labor law and labor welfare.
7. Abnormal psychology.
8. Criminology and penology.
9. Administration of a social agency.
10. Supervision in social work.
11. Economic demography.
12. Dynamics of population growth and family planning, including sex education.
13. Rehabilitation of the disabled and deviant.
14. Urban and rural community development.
15. Seminars on family, child, youth and workers' welfare.
16. Clinical psychology.

The subjects covered in the M.A. program are:
1. Social welfare administration.
2. Social policy and planning: regional.
3. Social policy and planning: national.
4. Social and community development.
5. Research and social surveys.
6. Economic and social changes in Iran.
7. Seminars on social problems of Iran.
8. Applied social work: casework, group work and community work.
9. Social policy and planning in the fields of family, child, youth and workers' welfare.
10. Dynamics of population growth and family planning.
11. Laws affecting children, youth and family.
12. Review of psychology.
13. Psychotherapy.
14. Social pathology.
15. Statistics for social research.

16. Problems in public health.
17. Seminars in supervision.
18. Organizational development.
19. Thesis.
20. Teaching techniques and staff development.

Notes

Chapter I

[1]Most of the information in chapter I comes from Majid Tehranian, "Iran," Abid A. Al-Marayati and others, *The Middle East: Its Governments and Politics*, Belmont, California: Duxbury Press, 1972, pp. 401–14.

[2]Yahya Armajani, *Iran*, Englewood Cliffs, N.J.: Prentice-Hall, Inc., 1972, p. 57.

[3]A. Reza Arasteh and Josephine Arasteh, *Man and Society in Iran*, Leiden: E. J. Brill, 1970, p. 57.

[4]Harvey H. Smith *et al*, *Area Handbook for Iran*, Washington, D.C.: U. S. Government Printing Office, 1971, p. 209.

[5]Tehranian, *op. cit.*, p. 408.

[6]Donald N. Wilber, *Iran Past and Present*, Princeton: Princeton University Press, 1967, p. 1.

[7]E. S. Bayne, *Persian Kinship in Transition*, New York: American Universities Field Staff, Inc., 1968, p. 117.

[8]Richard N. Frye, *The Heritage of Persia*, New York: New American Library, 1966, pp. 27-28.

[9]Tehranian, *op. cit.*, p. 402.

[10]Arasteh and Arasteh, *op. cit.*, p. 13.

[11]Tehranian, *op. cit.*, pp. 401–408, 414.

[12]Wilber, *op. cit.*, pp. 6–7.

[13]*Ibid.*, p. 10.

[14]Arasteh and Arasteh, *op. cit.*, p. 2.

[15]*IranToday*, Teheran: Ministry of Foreign Affairs, 1973, p. 14. As is true in most developing countries, the statistical information is not always consistent or reliable.

[16]Shahpour Rassekh, "Planning for Social Change," in *Iran Faces the Seventies* (Ehsan Yar-Shatar, ed.), New York: Praeger, 1971, p. 151.

[17]John K. Friesen and Richard V. Moore, *Country Profiles: Iran*, New York: The Population Council, October 1972, p. 4.

[18]Plan and Budget Organization, The Imperial Government of Iran, *Summary of the Fifth National Development Plan, 1973-1978*, June, 1973, p. 7.

[19]E. S. Bayne, *op. cit.*, p. 170.

[20]Friesen and Moore, *op. cit.*, p. 3.

[21]W. Hardy Wickwar, "Food and Social Development in the Middle East," *The Middle East Journal*, Vol. 19, No. 2, Spring 1965, p. 183.

[22]Arasteh and Arasteh, *op. cit.*, p. 133. They cite an unpublished report issued by Plan Organization of Iran in 1959, "Social Conditions in Iran."

CHAPTER II

[1]The primary source for this chapter has been Ann K. S. Lambton's authoritative work, *Landlord and Peasant in Persia*, London: Oxford University Press, 1953. For village conditions, see also Arasteh and Arasteh, *Man and Society in Iran, op. cit.*, pp. 18-20; William C. Haas, *Iran*, New York: Columbia University Press, 1946, p. 196, 200, 231; Harvey H. Smith *et al, Area Handbook for Iran*, Washington, D.C.: U. S. Government Printing Office, 1971, pp. 116-17.

[2]Haas, *op. cit.*, p. 196.

[3]It should be noted that the landlord system is hundreds of years old in Iran, and improvements have occurred in recent times.

[4]Lambton, *op. cit.*, pp. 267-69

[5]*Ibid.*, p. 271.

[6]Bayne, *op. cit.*, p. 130.

[7]Lambton,*op. cit.*, pp. 239-240.

[8]*Ibid.*, p. 238.

[9]*Ibid.*, p. 246.

[10]*Ibid.*, p. 252.

[11]*Ibid.*, p. 234. Lambton errs in stating that the Shah Cheragh Mosque is in Teheran.

[12]*Ibid.*, p. 295.

[13]*Ibid.*, p. 302.

[14]*Ibid.*, p. 331.

[15]*Ibid.*, p. 334–35.

[16]*Ibid.*, pp. 337–49.

[17]*Ibid.*, p. 302, p. 375.

[18]*Ibid.*, p. 375.

[19]*Ibid.*, pp. 380–84.

[20]*Ibid.*, p. 387.

[21]In addition to Lambton and Arasteh and Arasteh, see the following books for descriptions of village life: John Shearman, *The Land and People of Iran*, London: Adam and Charles Black, 1962, pp. 41–46; Joseph M. Upton, *The History of Modern Iran: An Interpretation*, Cambridge, Mass.: Harvard University Press, 1961, pp. 64–80; and Donald N. Wilber, *Iran Past and Present*, Princeton: Princeton University Press, sixth ed., 1967, pp. 169–74.

[22]Lambton, *op. cit.*, p. 390.

[23]Information obtained from officials of the Ministry of Health, Government of Iran.

[24]Lambton, *op. cit.*, 390.

[25]Reza Arasteh, *Education and Social Awakening in Iran*, Leiden: E. J. Brill, 1962, pp. 13–15.

[26]*Iran Almanac and Book of Facts 1972*, Teheran: Echo of Iran, 1972, p. 543.

[27]Ann K. S. Lambton, *The Persian Land Reform: 1962– 1966*, Oxford: Clarendon Press, 1969, pp. 36–46.

[28]Smith *et al, op. cit.*, pp. 406–07.

[29]H. I. M. Mohammad Reza Pahlavi Aryamehr, Shahanshah of Iran, *The White Revolution of Iran*, Teheran: The Imperial Pahlavi Library, August 1967, p. 33.

[30]Smith *et al, op. cit.*, p. 407

[31]*Ibid.*

[32]Amin Banani, *The Modernization of Iran, 1921– 1941*, Stanford, California: Stanford University Press, 1961, pp. 143–44.

[33]*Ibid.*, p. 67.

[34]Wilber, *op. cit.*, p. 210.

[35]Banani, *op. cit.*, p. 86.

[36]*Ibid.*, pp. 92–93; see also Iranian Women's Association Yearbook, Teheran: Women's Association, 1966, p. 25 (in Persian).

[37]Wilber, *op. cit.*, p. 204.

[38]Ali Asghar Hekmat, *Ettela'at* (Persian language daily newspaper), Teheran, February 18, 1973, n.p.

[39]Friesen and Moore, *op. cit.*, p. 2.

40Bayne, *op. cit.*, p. 171.

41Paul Ward English, *City and Village in Iran: Settlement and Economy in the Kirman Basin*, Madison: The University of Wisconsin Press, 1966, p. 99.

42W. B. Fisher, ed., *The Cambridge History of Iran*, Vol. I, Cambridge: Cambridge University Press, 1968, p. 460.

43*Ibid.*, p. 665.

44Lambton, *Landlord and Peasant in Persia, op. cit.*, p. 288.

45Wilber, *op. cit.*, p. 169.

46Frederik Barth, *Nomads of South Persia*, Oslo, Norway: Oslo University Press, 1961, p. 120.

47Fisher, *op. cit.*, p. 640.

48Arasteh and Arasteh, *op. cit.*, pp. 142–43.

49*Iranian Women's Association Yearbook, op. cit.*, pp. 69–70.

50The foregoing information is excerpted from Jamshid Behnam and Shahpour Rosekh, *Introduction to the Sociology of Iran*, Teheran: Kharazmi, 1969, pp. 114–16 (written in Persian).

51On the role and status of women, see Arasteh and Arasteh, *op. cit., passim;* Haas, op. cit., pp. 160, 165; Behnam and Rosekh, *op. cit.*, pp. 114–16; *Iranian Women's Association Yearbook, op. cit.*, p. 70.

52S. G. Wilson, *Persian Life and Customs*, New York: Fleming H. Revell Company, 1895, p. 257.

53See Nader Afshar Naderi, "Discussion Paper on Husbands and Wives: Collaterals," presented at a Seminar on Modernization and Family Life in Mediterranean Society, Rome: Center for Mediterranean Studies, April 9–13, 1973, unpublished mimeograph.

54Arasteh and Arasteh, *op. cit.*, pp. 155–56.

CHAPTER III

1Smith *et al, op. cit.*, p. 287.

2Hafez F. Farmayan, "Politics During the Sixties: A Historical Analysis," *Iran Faces the Seventies* (Ehsan Yar-Shatar, ed.), New York: Praeger, 1971, p. 103. See also H.I.M. Mohammad Reza Pahlavi Aryamehr, Shahanshah of Iran, *The White Revolution of Iran, op. cit.*, pp. 3–4.

3Farmayan, *op. cit.*, p. 103.

4*Ibid.*, pp. 104–05.

5This quote and those that follow are taken from H.I.M. Mohammad Reza Pahlavi Aryamehr, *The White Revolution of Iran, op. cit.*, pp. 2, 3, 15, 17–18.

6Ramesh Sanghvi, *Aryamehr: The Shah of Iran*, New York: Stein and Day, 1968, p. 276.

[7]Smith *et al, op. cit.,* pp. 70–74, 286–89.

[8]Yahya Armajani, *op. cit.,* p. 171.

[9]Richard W. Cottam, *Nationalism in Iran,* Pittsburgh: University of Pittsburgh Press, 1964, p. 306.

[10]Rassekh, *op. cit.,* p. 160.

[11]Richard N. Frye, *Persia,* New York: Shocken Books, 1969, p. 105.

[12]Plan and Budget Organization, *Summary of the Fifth National Development Plan,* op. cit., p. 99.

[13]Tehranian, *op. cit.,* p. 411.

[14]Lambton, *The Persian Land Reform: 1962–1966, op. cit.,* p. 352.

[15]Armajani, *op. cit.,* p. 172.

[16]"Social Policy and Planning in National Development," *International Social Development Review,* No. 3, New York, United Nations, 1971, p. 7.

[17]Frye, *op. cit.,* p. 107.

[18]"The White Revolution and I," *Teheran Journal,* White Revolution Special, Teheran, January 21, 1973, pp. 11, 13, 15.

[19]Tehranian, *op. cit.,* p. 410.

[20]Plan and Budget Organization, *Summary of the Fifth Development Plan, op. cit.,* p. 123, p. 99.

[21]The strong preference of professionals for urban employment remains a serious problem today.

[22]Frye, *op. cit.,* pp. 108–09.

[23]"The White Revolution and I," *op. cit., passim.*

[24]Smith et al, *op. cit.,* pp. 287–89.

[25]Summarized from Herbert Kaufman, *The Limits of Organizational Change,* University, Alabama: The University of Alabama Press, 1971, Chapter 1.

[26]Marvin Zonis, *The Political Elite of Iran,* Princeton, N.J.: Princeton University Press, 1971, p. 14.

[27]Jon A. Teta, *Iran,* New York: Sterling Publishing Co., 1973, p. 37.

[28]*Ibid.*

[29]Smith et al, *op. cit.,* pp. 277–78.

[30]*Fourth National Development Plan 1968–1972,* Teheran: Plan Organization, 1968, p. 313.

[31]Plan and Budget Organization, *Summary of the Fifth National Development Plan, 1973–1978,* p. 1.

[32]*Fourth National Development Plan 1968–1972, op. cit.,* p. 313. Since publication, the Ministry of Labor and Social Affairs was divided into the present Ministry of Labor and Ministry of Social Welfare.

[33]*Ibid.*, p. 314.
[34]Smith *et al, op. cit.*, p. 372.
[35]*Fourth National Development Plan 1968–1972, op. cit.*, p. 321.
[36]*Summary of the Fifth National Development Plan, op. cit.*, pp. 142–51.
[37]These sections are adapted from the *Fourth National Development Plan*, pp. 325–27.

CHAPTER IV

[1]See, for example, Harold L. Wilensky and Charles N. Lebeaux, *Industrial Society and Social Welfare*, New York: The Free Press, 1958.
[2]M. Amani, *Overview of the Demographic Situation of Iran*, Teheran: University of Teheran Institute for Social Studies and Research, July 1971, 16 pp. mimeograph, p. 8.
[3]*Summary of The Fifth National Development Plan*, 1973–1978, p. 108.
[4]Philip Hauser refers to this phenomenon as the "revolution of rising expectations." Philip M. Hauser, *Population, Poverty and World Politics*, Urbana: University of Illinois Bulletin, Vol. 62, Number 97, June, 1965, p. 9.

CHAPTER V

[1]Hauser, *op. cit.*, p. 8.
[2]*Ibid.*, p. 16.
[3]*Summary of the Fifth Development Plan, 1973–1978, op. cit.*, pp. 136–37.
[4]Smith *et al, op. cit.*, pp. 85–86.
[5]*Summary of the Fifth Development Plan, 1973–1978, op. cit.*, p. 2.
[6]United Nations, *Population and Family Planning in Iran* (TAO/IRA /60), New York: United Nations, April 7, 1971, p. 34.
[7]Friesen and Moore, *op. cit.*, p. 2.
[8]*Population Projections for Iran*, International Demographic Statistics Center, Population Division, U.S. Bureau of the Census, October 9, 1970, 12 pp. unpublished mimeograph, p. 3.
[9]Friesen and Moore, *op. cit.*, p. 1.
[10]M. Amani, *op. cit.*, pp. 3, 7.
[11]Friesen and Moore, *op. cit.*, p. 11.
[12]In conversation with the author, Teheran, April 8, 1973.
[13]Friesen and Moore, *op. cit.*, p. 17.
[14]Farah Maternity Hospital was one of the first student placement

centers for the newly opened School of Social Work in 1958.

[15]It should be pointed out that residents of neighboring communities also take advantage of the clinical facilities.

[16]A KAP (knowledge, attitudes, practice) study was made by UNESCO in Teheran in 1971. Most women (96%), whether literate or not, believed in the possibility of birth control. Their ideals concerning family size ranged from 2.9 for literate women to 3.2 for illiterate women. This is in marked contrast to the actual size of families. Among them, 57.7 percent reported using some form of contraception (69.9 percent of literates and 45.8 percent of illiterates), although withdrawal was the preferred method among 46% of the Teheran respondents. Less than one percent felt birth control was never justified. The majority of married women (63%) felt that birth control and family planning were acceptable within the Islamic religion. (See Friesen and Moore, *op. cit.*, pp. 4, 7.)

[17]See, for example, the KAP study made by UNESCO in 1971.

[18]John K. Friesen, *Country Profiles: Iran*, New York; The Population Council, December 1969, p. 2.

[19]*Address of the Shahanshah Aryamehr and Reports by the Prime Minister and the Plan Organization Managing Director*, Teheran: The Imperial Government of Iran, 29 December 1970, pp. 32–33.

[20]Friesen and Moore, *op. cit.*, p. 13.

[21]*Ibid.*, p. 9.

[22]*Ibid.*, p. 10.

[23]*Statistics of Doctors and Dentists in Iran*, Vol. 2, Medical Association of Iran, 1971, p. 11 (in Persian), and Ali A. Paydarfar, *The Population and Family Planning Programme in Iran*, Chapel Hill: The University of North Carolina, March 1972, pp. 26–27.

[24]Friesen and Moore, *op. cit.*, p. 11.

[25]Paydarfar, *op. cit.*, p. 41.

[26]*Ibid.*, p. 43.

[27]Friesen and Moore, *op. cit.*, p. 11.

[28]*Ibid.*

[29]Paydarfar, *op. cit.*, p. 66.

[30]Friesen and Moore, *op. cit.*, p. 12.

Chapter VI

[1]Free use of a building for the center was donated by the United Presbyterian Church in the United States in 1970.

[2]See *Summary of the Fifth National Development Plan, 1973–1978*, *op. cit.*, p. 147.

³The distinction between an institutional or development conception of social welfare on the one hand and a residual conception on the other was first articulated in the social work literature by Harold L. Wilensky and Charles N. Lebeaux in *Industrial Society and Social Welfare* in 1958. See the more recent paperback edition, New York: The Free Press, 1965, pp. 138–138. They describe the residual conception as a temporary substitute when the normal structures, such as family and market, break down, and the institutional conception as a permanent, normal, first-line function of modern industrial society. Thus, family services to parents having marital troubles or public assistance to a poor person are examples of the residual conception. Social security, public health, and public education are normal services available to the total, or nearly total, population and are examples of the institutional conception.

⁴The Naziabad Center was visited by the author and the visit was recorded by him.

⁵Since the 1972 visit, the government has enacted a retirement plan affecting these employees.

Chapter VII

¹Personal interview by the author with former Mayor Musa Mohan, on May 28, 1973.

²Statement made to the author by Mr. Kazem Zamoni, Director of Child Center 3 of the Municipality of Teheran, on May 7, 1973.

³The following information was obtained in a personal interview by the author with Mr. Bagher Ameli on April 9, 1973.

⁴*Teheran School of Social Work: Report of the Ten-Year Activities*, Teheran: 1969, p. 23 (in Persian).

⁵See note 3.

⁶Information in this section was received by the author in an interview on June 4, 1973 with Mrs. Soráya Sepahai, Deputy Director, National Iranian Society for the Rehabilitation of the Disabled.

⁷F. Rahim, "Getting to Know the Social Worker's Activity in Arj Factory," *Social Worker* (monthly newsletter of Iran Society of Social Workers), Teheran: March 1964. (In Persian).

⁸*Teheran School of Social Work: Report of the Ten-Year Activities*, op. cit., p. 37.

Chapter VIII

¹See, for example, Robert Perlman and Arnold Gurin, *Community*

Organization and Social Planning, N.Y.: John Wiley and Sons, Inc., 1972, pp. 102–08.

²*Ibid.*, p. 261, p. 272.

³See Allen Pincus and Anne Minahan, *Social Worker Practice: Model and Method*, Itasca, Illinois: F. E. Peacock, Inc., 1973, p. 15.

⁴*Fourth National Development Plan, op. cit.*, pp. 237–39.

⁵*Summary of the Fifth National Development Plan, 1973–1978*, p. 101.

⁶See "Rural Community Development and Planning: Promise and Reality," *International Social Development Review*, No. 2, New York: United Nations, 1970, p. 31.

CHAPTER IX

¹Smith, *et al, op. cit.*, pp. 145–47.

²*Iranshahr*, Teheran: UNESCO, Vol. II, No. 22, 1964, p. 1,445.

³Smith, *op. cit.*, p. 151.

⁴*A Record of Twenty Years of Services to People by the Imperial Organization for Social Services*, 1947–1967, Teheran: 1967, p. 6.

⁵Smith, *op. cit.*, p. 150.

⁶*Ibid.*

⁷*Ibid.*, p. 151.

⁸*Iranshahr, op. cit.*, p. 1, 987. See also *Third National Development Plan*, Teheran: Plan Organization, 1965.

⁹All college and university education in Iran comes under the jurisdiction of the Ministry of Science and Higher Education which grants charters and degrees. Thus, a number of independent colleges exist and are allowed to confer degrees under the auspices of the Ministry. The Teheran School of Social Work functions autonomously with an independent board of trustees, rather than with the university affiliation common to schools of social work in most countries. This arrangement allows the School to retain control over such matters as curriculum development, field instruction, faculty appointments, and budgetary allocations. However, serving as permanent board members and advising the School are the Chancellor of Teheran University and five cabinet ministers. The full list of board members is provided in text.

¹⁰See Chart I for the growth of the student body.

¹¹Margaret Hardiman, "Social Structure and Social Policy in Less Developed Countries," *Assignment Children*, United Nation's Children's Fund, July-September 1972, p. 95.

¹²For a discussion of the impact of job on social workers' values see

Charles S. Levy, "The Value Base of Social Work," *Journal of Education for Social Work*, Vol. 9, No. 1, Winter 1973, p. 36.

[13]Frederick Harbison and Charles A. Myers, *Education, Manpower, and Economic Growth*, New York: McGraw-Hill, 1964, p. 186.

[14]Herman D. Stein, "Professions and Universities," *Journal of Education for Social Work*, Vol. 4, No. 2, Fall 1968, p. 60.

[15]*Population Projections for Iran, op. cit.*

[16]M. Amani, *op. cit.*, p. 5.

[17]"Social Policy and Planning In National Development," *International Social Development Review*, No. 3, N.Y.: United Nations, 1971, p. 8.

[18]In 1967, the Ministry of Education was reorganized into two ministries, and the Teheran School of Social Work was placed under one of them, the Ministry of Science and Higher Education.

[19]See His Imperial Majesty Mohammed Reza Shah Pahlavi, Shahanshah of Iran, *Mission For My Country*, New York: McGraw-Hill Book Company, Inc., 1961, pp. 185 ff.

[20]For example, see Eileen A. Blackey, "Patterns of Social Work Education in Meeting the Needs of Societies," *International Social Work*, Vol. XIII, No. 3, 1970, p. 13.

[21]Hans Nagpaul, "The Diffusion of American Social Work Education to India: Problems and Issues," *International Social Work*, Vol. XV, No. 1, 1972, p. 3; A. Shawky, "Social Work Education in Africa," *International Social Work*, Vol. XV, No. 3, 1972, pp. 12-13.

[22]Nagpaul, *op. cit.*, p. 15.

[23]See Daniel S. Sanders, "Social Aspects of Economic Policy and Development," *International Social Work*, Vol. XV, No. 3, 1972, p. 30.

CHAPTER X

[1]See, for example, Roy Lubove, *The Professional Altruist*, Cambridge, Massachusetts: Harvard University Press, 1965, Chapter 1, especially page 5.

[2]For example, see Roy Lubove, editor, *Social Welfare in Transition*, Pittsburgh: University of Pittsburgh Press, 1966, pp. 41–44, 197–334.

[3]See James Alban Bill, *The Politics of Iran*, Columbus, Ohio: Charles E. Merrill Publishing Co., 1972, p. 9. He discusses the "thousand families" important in Iran as really more like one to two hundred, and specifically names the "Farmanfarmaiyan" family as one of those that continues to retain upper-class status.

[4]See Footnote 3, Page 184, for a clarification of the terms "Institution-

al" and "Developmental."

[5]*Summary of the Fifth National Development Plan, 1973–1798, op. cit.*, p. 137.

[6]*Ibid.*, pp. 139–40.

[7]*Ibid.*, p. 150.

CHAPTER XI

[1]Zonis, *op. cit.*, p. 335

[2]*The Teheran Journal*, September 23, 1974, p. 3.

[3]*Ibid.*, October 6, 1974, p. 1.

[4]*Ibid.*, October 1, 1974.

[5]*Ibid.*, October 6, 1974, p. 1.

[6]*Kayhan International*, May 12, 1974, p. 4.

[7]Zonis, *op. cit.*, p. 339.

[8]Bill, *op. cit.*, p. 155.

[9]Bayne, *op. cit.*, p. 247.

[10]Lewis M. Simons, "Shah's Dreams are Outpacing Iran's Economic Boom," *The Washington Post*, Sunday, May 26, 1974, p. A 6.

[11]*Ibid.*

[12]Ali A. Paydarfar, *Demographic Consequences of Modernization: A Population Analysis of Iran and Comparison with Selected Nations*, Washington, D.C.: International Research Institute, American Institutes for Research, 1967, p. 133.

[13]*Kayhan International*, September 24, 1974, p. 2.

[14]*Ibid.*, October 20, 1974, p. 4.

[15]*Ibid.*, September 26, 1974, p. 2.

[16]*Ibid.*, May 12, 1974, p. 4.

[17]Philip Hauser has called attention to the fact that "poverty and frustration concentrated in the urban setting have a potential for generating social unrest, political instability, and threats to world peace of a much greater magnitude than poverty and frustration dispersed widely over the countryside." Philip M. Hauser, *op. cit.*, p. 13.

[18]Arasteh, *op. cit.*, pp. 178–80.

[19]The Iranian Government's position on planning, for example, can be understood from the statement in the Fifth Development plan that 100 social planning experts will be trained at the post-graduate level. *Summary of the Fifth National Development Plan, 1973–1978*, p. 150.

[20]Pahlavi, *op. cit.*, p. 21.

[21]Raanan Weitz, "Social Planning in Rural Regional Development: The Israeli Experience," *International Social Development Review*, No. 4. New York: United Nations, 1972, p. 58.

Selected Bibliography

Al-Marayati, Abid A. and others. *The Middle East: Its Governments and Politics*, Belmont, California: Duxbury Press, 1972.

Amani, M. *Overview of the Demographic Situation of Iran*, Teheran: University of Teheran, Institute for Social Studies, July 1971 (mimeograph).

Arasteh, A. Reza. *Man and Society in Iran*, Leiden: E. J. Brill, 1964.

Arasteh, Reza and Josephine. *Man and Society in Iran*, Leiden: E. J. Brill, 1970.

Bayne, E. A. *Persian Kinship in Transition*, New York: American Universities Field Staff, Inc., 1968.

Behnam, Jamshid and Rosekh, Shahpour. *Introduction to the Sociology of Iran*, Teheran: Kharamsi, 1969 (in Persian).

Cottam, Richard W. *Nationalism in Iran*, Pittsburgh: University of Pittsburgh Press, 1964.

Fisher, W. B., ed. *The Cambridge History of Iran*, Vol. 1, Cambridge: Cambridge University Press, 1968.

Friesen, John K. and Moore, Richard V. *Country Profiles: Iran*, New York: The Population Council, October 1972.

H. I. M. Mohammed Reza Pahlavi Aryamehr, Shahanshah of Iran. *Mission for My Country*, New York: McGraw-Hill Book Company, Inc., 1961.

H. I. M. Mohammed Reza Pahlavi Aryamehr, Shahanshah of Iran, *The White Revolution of Iran*, Teheran: The Imperial Pahlavi Library, August 1967.

Lambton, Ann K. S. *Landlord and Peasant in Persia,* London: Oxford University Press, 1953.

Lambton, Ann K. S. *The Persian Land Reform, 1962-1966,* Oxford: Clarendon Press, 1969.

Paydarfar, Ali A. *The Population and Family Planning Programme in Iran,* Chapel Hill: The University of North Carolina, March 1972.

Plan Organization of Iran. *Fourth National Development Plan, 1968-1972,* Teheran, 1968.

Plan Organization of Iran. *Summary of the Fifth National Development Plan, 1973–1978,* Teheran, 1973.

Sanghvi, Ramesh. *Aryamehr: The Shah of Iran,* London: Transorient Books, Ltd., 1968.

Smith, Harvey H. *et al. Area Handbook for Iran,* Washington, D.C.: U. S. Government Printing Office, 1971.

Teheran Journal, "White Revolution and I" (special supplement), Teheran: Ettela'at Publications, January 21, 1973.

Teheran School of Social Work. *Bulletin,* Teheran: 1972.

Wilber, Donald N. *Iran Past and Present,* Princeton: Princeton University Press, sixth edition, 1967.

Yar-Shatar, Ehsan, ed. *Iran Faces the Seventies,* New York: Praeger, 1971.

Zonis, Marvin. *The Political Elite of Iran,* Princeton, N. J.: Princeton University Press, 1971.

Index

191